50% OFF Online OAE Foundati Prep Course!

Dear Customer,

We consider it an honor and a privilege that you chose our OAE Study Guide. As a way of showing our appreciation and to help us better serve you, we have partnered with Mometrix Test Preparation to offer you **50% off their online OAE Foundations of Reading Prep Course**. Many Foundations of Reading courses are needlessly expensive and don't deliver enough value. With their course, you get access to the best OAE Foundations of Reading prep material, and **you only pay half price**.

Mometrix has structured their online course to perfectly complement your printed study guide. The OAE Foundations of Reading Prep Course contains **in-depth lessons** that cover all the most important topics, **40+ video reviews** that explain difficult concepts, over **400 practice questions** to ensure you feel prepared, and **300+ digital flashcards**, so you can study while you're on the go.

Online OAE Foundations of Reading Prep Course

Topics Included:

- Foundations of Reading Development
  - Vocabulary Development and Word Analysis
  - Morphology
- Development of Reading Comprehension
  - Writing Development
  - Oral Language Acquisition and Development
- Reading Assessment and Instruction
  - Learning Environments that Support Reading
  - Diverse Learners and Specific Needs

Course Features:

- OAE Study Guide
  - Get content that complements our best-selling study guide.
- Full-Length Practice Tests
  - With over 400 practice questions, you can test yourself again and again.
- Mobile Friendly
  - If you need to study on the go, the course is easily accessible from your mobile device.
- OAE Foundations of Reading Flashcards
  - Their course includes a flashcard mode with over 300 content cards to help you study.

To receive this discount, visit them at mometrix.com/university/oae-reading or simply scan this QR code with your smartphone. At the checkout page, enter the discount code: **TPBOAE50**

If you have any questions or concerns, please don't hesitate to contact Mometrix at support@mometrix.com.

Sincerely,

 in partnership with

FREE Test Taking Tips Video/DVD Offer

To better serve you, we created videos covering test taking tips that we want to give you for FREE. **These videos cover world-class tips that will help you succeed on your test.**

We just ask that you send us feedback about this product. Please let us know what you thought about it—whether good, bad, or indifferent.

To get your **FREE videos**, you can use the QR code below or email freevideos@studyguideteam.com with "Free Videos" in the subject line and the following information in the body of the email:

      a. The title of your product

      b. Your product rating on a scale of 1-5, with 5 being the highest

      c. Your feedback about the product

If you have any questions or concerns, please don't hesitate to contact us at info@studyguideteam.com.

Thank you!

OAE Foundations of Reading 190 Study Guide

Test Prep and Practice Exam for the Ohio Assessment for Educators
[Updated for the New Outline]

Lydia Morrison

Written and edited by TPB Publishing.

TPB Publishing is not associated with or endorsed by any official testing organization. TPB Publishing is a publisher of unofficial educational products. All test and organization names are trademarks of their respective owners. Content in this book is included for utilitarian purposes only and does not constitute an endorsement by TPB Publishing of any particular point of view.

Interested in buying more than 10 copies of our product? Contact us about bulk discounts:
bulkorders@studyguideteam.com

ISBN 13: 9781637754030

Table of Contents

Welcome

Dear Reader,

Welcome to your new Test Prep Books study guide! We are pleased that you chose us to help you prepare for your exam. There are many study options to choose from, and we appreciate you choosing us. Studying can be a daunting task, but we have designed a smart, effective study guide to help prepare you for what lies ahead.

Whether you're a parent helping your child learn and grow, a high school student working hard to get into your dream college, or a nursing student studying for a complex exam, we want to help give you the tools you need to succeed. We hope this study guide gives you the skills and the confidence to thrive, and we can't thank you enough for allowing us to be part of your journey.

In an effort to continue to improve our products, we welcome feedback from our customers. We look forward to hearing from you. Suggestions, success stories, and criticisms can all be communicated by emailing us at info@studyguideteam.com.

Sincerely,
Test Prep Books Team

FREE Videos/DVD OFFER

Doing well on your exam requires both knowing the test content and understanding how to use that knowledge to do well on the test. We offer completely FREE test taking tip videos. **These videos cover world-class tips that you can use to succeed on your test.**

To get your **FREE videos**, you can use the QR code below or email freevideos@studyguideteam.com with "Free Videos" in the subject line and the following information in the body of the email:

   a. The title of your product
   b. Your product rating on a scale of 1-5, with 5 being the highest
   c. Your feedback about the product

If you have any questions or concerns, please don't hesitate to contact us at info@studyguideteam.com.

SCAN HERE

Quick Overview

As you draw closer to taking your exam, effective preparation becomes more and more important. Thankfully, you have this study guide to help you get ready. Use this guide to help keep your studying on track and refer to it often.

This study guide contains several key sections that will help you be successful on your exam. The guide contains tips for what you should do the night before and the day of the test. Also included are test-taking tips. Knowing the right information is not always enough. Many well-prepared test takers struggle with exams. These tips will help equip you to accurately read, assess, and answer test questions.

A large part of the guide is devoted to showing you what content to expect on the exam and to helping you better understand that content. In this guide are practice test questions so that you can see how well you have grasped the content. Then, answer explanations are provided so that you can understand why you missed certain questions.

Don't try to cram the night before you take your exam. This is not a wise strategy for a few reasons. First, your retention of the information will be low. Your time would be better used by reviewing information you already know rather than trying to learn a lot of new information. Second, you will likely become stressed as you try to gain a large amount of knowledge in a short amount of time. Third, you will be depriving yourself of sleep. So be sure to go to bed at a reasonable time the night before. Being well-rested helps you focus and remain calm.

Be sure to eat a substantial breakfast the morning of the exam. If you are taking the exam in the afternoon, be sure to have a good lunch as well. Being hungry is distracting and can make it difficult to focus. You have hopefully spent lots of time preparing for the exam. Don't let an empty stomach get in the way of success!

When travelling to the testing center, leave earlier than needed. That way, you have a buffer in case you experience any delays. This will help you remain calm and will keep you from missing your appointment time at the testing center.

Be sure to pace yourself during the exam. Don't try to rush through the exam. There is no need to risk performing poorly on the exam just so you can leave the testing center early. Allow yourself to use all of the allotted time if needed.

 Remain positive while taking the exam even if you feel like you are performing poorly. Thinking about the content you should have mastered will not help you perform better on the exam.

Once the exam is complete, take some time to relax. Even if you feel that you need to take the exam again, you will be well served by some down time before you begin studying again. It's often easier to convince yourself to study if you know that it will come with a reward!

Test-Taking Strategies

1. Predicting the Answer

When you feel confident in your preparation for a multiple-choice test, try predicting the answer before reading the answer choices. This is especially useful on questions that test objective factual knowledge. By predicting the answer before reading the available choices, you eliminate the possibility that you will be distracted or led astray by an incorrect answer choice. You will feel more confident in your selection if you read the question, predict the answer, and then find your prediction among the answer choices. After using this strategy, be sure to still read all of the answer choices carefully and completely. If you feel unprepared, you should not attempt to predict the answers. This would be a waste of time and an opportunity for your mind to wander in the wrong direction.

2. Reading the Whole Question

Too often, test takers scan a multiple-choice question, recognize a few familiar words, and immediately jump to the answer choices. Test authors are aware of this common impatience, and they will sometimes prey upon it. For instance, a test author might subtly turn the question into a negative, or he or she might redirect the focus of the question right at the end. The only way to avoid falling into these traps is to read the entirety of the question carefully before reading the answer choices.

3. Looking for Wrong Answers

Long and complicated multiple-choice questions can be intimidating. One way to simplify a difficult multiple-choice question is to eliminate all of the answer choices that are clearly wrong. In most sets of answers, there will be at least one selection that can be dismissed right away. If the test is administered on paper, the test taker could draw a line through it to indicate that it may be ignored; otherwise, the test taker will have to perform this operation mentally or on scratch paper. In either case, once the obviously incorrect answers have been eliminated, the remaining choices may be considered. Sometimes identifying the clearly wrong answers will give the test taker some information about the correct answer. For instance, if one of the remaining answer choices is a direct opposite of one of the eliminated answer choices, it may well be the correct answer. The opposite of obviously wrong is obviously right! Of course, this is not always the case. Some answers are obviously incorrect simply because they are irrelevant to the question being asked. Still, identifying and eliminating some incorrect answer choices is a good way to simplify a multiple-choice question.

4. Don't Overanalyze

Anxious test takers often overanalyze questions. When you are nervous, your brain will often run wild, causing you to make associations and discover clues that don't actually exist. If you feel that this may be a problem for you, do whatever you can to slow down during the test. Try taking a deep breath or counting to ten. As you read and consider the question, restrict yourself to the particular words used by the author. Avoid thought tangents about what the author *really* meant, or what he or she was *trying* to say. The only things that matter on a multiple-choice test are the words that are actually in the question. You must avoid reading too much into a multiple-choice question, or supposing that the writer meant something other than what he or she wrote.

3

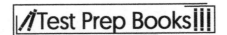

5. No Need for Panic

It is wise to learn as many strategies as possible before taking a multiple-choice test, but it is likely that you will come across a few questions for which you simply don't know the answer. In this situation, avoid panicking. Because most multiple-choice tests include dozens of questions, the relative value of a single wrong answer is small. As much as possible, you should compartmentalize each question on a multiple-choice test. In other words, you should not allow your feelings about one question to affect your success on the others. When you find a question that you either don't understand or don't know how to answer, just take a deep breath and do your best. Read the entire question slowly and carefully. Try rephrasing the question a couple of different ways. Then, read all of the answer choices carefully. After eliminating obviously wrong answers, make a selection and move on to the next question.

6. Confusing Answer Choices

When working on a difficult multiple-choice question, there may be a tendency to focus on the answer choices that are the easiest to understand. Many people, whether consciously or not, gravitate to the answer choices that require the least concentration, knowledge, and memory. This is a mistake. When you come across an answer choice that is confusing, you should give it extra attention. A question might be confusing because you do not know the subject matter to which it refers. If this is the case, don't  eliminate the answer before you have affirmatively settled on another. When you come across an answer choice of this type, set it aside as you look at the remaining choices. If you can confidently assert that one of the other choices is correct, you can leave the confusing answer aside. Otherwise, you will need to take a moment to try to better understand the confusing answer choice. Rephrasing is one way to tease out the sense of a confusing answer choice.

7. Your First Instinct

Many people struggle with multiple-choice tests because they overthink the questions. If you have studied sufficiently for the test, you should be prepared to trust your first instinct once you have carefully and completely read the question and all of the answer choices. There is a great deal of research suggesting that the mind can come to the correct conclusion very quickly once it has obtained all of the relevant information. At times, it may seem to you as if your intuition is working faster even than your reasoning mind. This may in fact be true. The knowledge you obtain while studying may be retrieved from your subconscious before you have a chance to work out the associations that support it. Verify your instinct by working out the reasons that it should be trusted.

8. Key Words

Many test takers struggle with multiple-choice questions because they have poor reading comprehension skills. Quickly reading and understanding a multiple-choice question requires a mixture of skill and experience. To help with this, try jotting down a few key words and phrases on a piece of scrap paper. Doing this concentrates the process of reading and forces the mind to weigh the relative importance of the question's parts. In selecting words and phrases to write down, the test taker thinks

4

about the question more deeply and carefully. This is especially true for multiple-choice questions that are preceded by a long prompt.

9. Subtle Negatives

One of the oldest tricks in the multiple-choice test writer's book is to subtly reverse the meaning of a question with a word like *not* or *except*. If you are not paying attention to each word in the question, you can easily be led astray by this trick. For instance, a common question format is, "Which of the following is...?" Obviously, if the question instead is, "Which of the following is not...?," then the answer will be quite different. Even worse, the test makers are aware of the potential for this mistake and will include one answer choice that would be correct if the question were not negated or reversed. A test taker who misses the reversal will find what he or she believes to be a correct answer and will be so confident that he or she will fail to reread the question and discover the original error. The only way to avoid this is to practice a wide variety of multiple-choice questions and to pay close attention to each and every word.

10. Reading Every Answer Choice

It may seem obvious, but you should always read every one of the answer choices! Too many test takers fall into the habit of scanning the question and assuming that they understand the question because they recognize a few key words. From there, they pick the first answer choice that answers the question they believe they have read. Test takers who read all of the answer choices might discover that one of the latter answer choices is actually *more* correct. Moreover, reading all of the answer choices can remind you of facts related to the question that can help you arrive at the correct answer. Sometimes, a misstatement or incorrect detail in one of the latter answer choices will trigger your memory of the subject and will enable you to find the right answer. Failing to read all of the answer choices is like not reading all of the items on a restaurant menu: you might miss out on the perfect choice.

11. Spot the Hedges

One of the keys to success on multiple-choice tests is paying close attention to every word. This is never truer than with words like *almost*, *most*, *some*, and *sometimes*. These words are called "hedges" because they indicate that a statement is not totally true or not true in every place and time. An absolute statement will contain no hedges, but in many subjects, the answers are not always straightforward or absolute. There are always exceptions to the rules in these subjects. For this reason,

you should favor those multiple-choice questions that contain hedging language. The presence of qualifying words indicates that the author is taking special care with his or her words, which is certainly important when composing the right answer. After all, there are many ways to be wrong, but there is only one way to be right! For this reason, it is wise to avoid answers that are absolute when taking a multiple-choice test. An absolute answer is one that says things are either all one way or all another. They often include words like *every*, *always*, *best*, and *never*. If you are taking a multiple-choice test in a subject that doesn't lend itself to absolute answers, be on your guard if you see any of these words.

12. Long Answers

 In many subject areas, the answers are not simple. As already mentioned, the right answer often requires hedges. Another common feature of the answers to a complex or subjective question are qualifying clauses, which are groups of words that subtly modify the meaning of the sentence. If the question or answer choice describes a rule to which there are exceptions or the subject matter is complicated, ambiguous, or confusing, the correct answer will require many words in order to be expressed clearly and accurately. In essence, you should not be deterred by answer choices that seem excessively long. Oftentimes, the author of the text will not be able to write the correct answer without offering some qualifications and modifications. Your job is to read the answer choices thoroughly and completely and to select the one that most accurately and precisely answers the question.

13. Restating to Understand

Sometimes, a question on a multiple-choice test is difficult not because of what it asks but because of how it is written. If this is the case, restate the question or answer choice in different words. This process serves a couple of important purposes. First, it forces you to concentrate on the core of the question. In order to rephrase the question accurately, you have to understand it well. Rephrasing the question will concentrate your mind on the key words and ideas. Second, it will present the information to your mind in a fresh way. This process may trigger your memory and render some useful scrap of information picked up while studying.

14. True Statements

Sometimes an answer choice will be true in itself, but it does not answer the question. This is one of the main reasons why it is essential to read the question carefully and completely before proceeding to the answer choices. Too often, test takers skip ahead to the answer choices and look for true statements. Having found one of these, they are content to select it without reference to the question above. The savvy test taker will always read the entire question before turning to the answer choices. Then, having settled on a correct answer choice, he or she will refer to the original question and ensure that the selected answer is relevant. The mistake of choosing a correct-but-irrelevant answer choice is especially common on questions related to specific pieces of objective knowledge.

15. No Patterns

One of the more dangerous ideas that circulates about multiple-choice tests is that the correct answers tend to fall into patterns. These erroneous ideas range from a belief that B and C are the most common right answers, to the idea that an unprepared test-taker should answer "A-B-A-C-A-D-A-B-A." It cannot be emphasized enough that pattern-seeking of this type is exactly the WRONG way to approach a multiple-choice test. To begin with, it is highly unlikely that the test maker will plot the correct answers according to some predetermined pattern. The questions are scrambled and delivered in a random order. Furthermore, even if the test maker was following a pattern in the assignation of correct answers, there is no reason why the test taker would know which pattern he or she was using. Any attempt to discern a pattern in the answer choices is a waste of time and a distraction from the real work of taking the test. A test taker would be much better served by extra preparation before the test than by reliance on a pattern in the answers.

Study Prep Plan

1 **Schedule** - Use one of our study schedules below or come up with one of your own.

2 **Relax** - Test anxiety can hurt even the best students. There are many ways to reduce stress. Find the one that works best for you.

3 **Execute** - Once you have a good plan in place, be sure to stick to it.

One Week Study Schedule		
Day 1	Subarea I - Foundations of Reading...	
Day 2	Role of Phonics in Promoting Reading...	
Day 3	Word Analysis Skills and Strategies	
Day 4	Subarea II - Development of Reading...	
Day 5	Subarea III - Reading Assessment...	
Day 6	Practice Test	
Day 7	Take Your Exam!	

Two Week Study Schedule			
Day 1	Subarea I - Foundations of Reading...	Day 8	Subarea III - Reading Assessment...
Day 2	Role of Phonics in Promoting Reading...	Day 9	Approaches to Reading Instruction
Day 3	Promoting Automaticity and Fluency	Day 10	Close Reading and Rereading
Day 4	Word Analysis Skills and Strategies	Day 11	Subarea IV - Integration of Knowledg...
Day 5	Subarea II - Developmen...	Day 12	Practice Test
Day 6	Imaginative and Literary Texts	Day 13	Answer Explanations
Day 7	Informational and Expository Texts	Day 14	Take Your Exam!

One Month Study Schedule					
Day 1	Subarea I - Foundations...	Day 11	Practice Questions	Day 21	Group Versus Individual Reading Assessments
Day 2	Print and the Alphabetic Principle	Day 12	Subarea II - Development...	Day 22	Approaches to Reading Instruction
Day 3	Strategies to Develop Letter Recognition	Day 13	Selecting Vocabulary Words	Day 23	Differentiating Reading Instruction
Day 4	Role of Phonics in Promoting Reading...	Day 14	Imaginative and Literary Texts	Day 24	Evaluating and Sequencing Texts...
Day 5	Stages of Spelling Development	Day 15	Reading Comprehension...	Day 25	Promoting Independent Reading in the...
Day 6	Use of Phonics Generalizations...	Day 16	Informational and Expository Texts	Day 26	Practice Questions
Day 7	Research-Based, Systematic, Explicit...	Day 17	Role of Reading Fluency in Informational...	Day 27	Subarea IV - Integration of Knowledge...
Day 8	Word Analysis Skills and Strategies	Day 18	Application of Comprehension...	Day 28	Practice Test
Day 9	Suffixes	Day 19	Practice Questions	Day 29	Answer Explanations
Day 10	Context Clues	Day 20	Subarea III - Reading Assessment...	Day 30	Take Your Exam!

Build your own prep plan by visiting:

testprepbooks.com/prep

As you study for your test, we'd like to take the opportunity to remind you that you are capable of great things! With the right tools and dedication, you truly can do anything you set your mind to. The fact that you are holding this book right now shows how committed you are. In case no one has told you lately, you've got this! Our intention behind including this coloring page is to give you the chance to take some time to engage your creative side when you need a little brain-break from studying. As a company, we want to encourage people like you to achieve their dreams by providing good quality study materials for the tests and certifications that improve careers and change lives. As individuals, many of us have taken such tests in our careers, and we know how challenging this process can be. While we can't come alongside you and cheer you on personally, we can offer you the space to recall your purpose, reconnect with your passion, and refresh your brain through an artistic practice. We wish you every success, and happy studying!

Introduction

Function of the Test

The Ohio Assessments for Educators (OAE) Foundations of Reading exam is for individuals who require licensure to teach in the state of Ohio. As of July 2017, the Foundations of Reading exam is required for the following licensing areas:

1. Early childhood

2. Middle childhood

3. Gifted

4. Mild/moderate educational needs

5. Moderate/intensive educational needs

6. Visually impaired

7. Hearing impaired

8. Early childhood intervention specialist

A passing test score on the OAE Foundations of Reading is one more step to becoming licensed for certain pedagogical areas in the state of Ohio.

Test Administration

The OAE Foundations of Reading assessment is offered year round by appointment through Pearson testing centers in Ohio and nationwide as a computer-based test. It is also given remotely as an online-proctored test. Those who wish to retake the assessment must reregister and wait a minimum of thirty days between tests. For those with disabilities unable to take the exam under standard conditions, nursing mothers, or those for whom English is a secondary language, alternative testing arrangements are provided with appropriate documentation submitted well before the exam date and approved by administration. Please visit the oh.nesinc.com website to learn more about testing with disabilities.

Test Format

The Foundations of Reading assessment is administered in Pearson testing sites around the nation and remotely. The exam is a computer-based test with 100 multiple-choice questions and two open-response written assignments; the test is four hours and fifteen minutes long when taken in-person. As an online-proctored test, the Foundations of Reading assessment is four hours and thirty minutes long, with two hours and thirty minutes for the multiple-choice section and one hour and thirty minutes for the written assignments with a fifteen-minute optional break in between. The subareas along with their test weight are noted below:

Multiple Choice
- Foundations of Reading Development (35%)

- Development of Reading Comprehension (27%)

- Reading Assessment and Instruction (18%)

<u>Open-Response</u>
- Foundational Reading Skills (10%)

- Reading Comprehension (10%)

Scoring

Score reports for the OAE Foundations of Reading can be mailed to test takers after the exam if they request this in their registration. The score will be available for two years in test taker accounts. The score report includes passing status, total score, and performance on competencies if you have taken more than one assessment. These reports are given to the Ohio Department of Education, the institution where you complete an educator preparation program, and any additional program providers you indicated on your registration. Possible scores are from 100 to 300 points. A passing score for the OAE Foundations of Reading is 220.

Subarea I—Foundations of Reading Development

Phonological and Phonemic Awareness

Phonological Awareness vs. Phonemic Awareness

Phonological awareness is the recognition that oral language is made of smaller units, such as syllables and words. **Phonemic awareness** is a type of phonological awareness. Phonemic-aware students recognize specific units of spoken language called phonemes. **Phonemes** are unique and easily identifiable units of sound. Examples include /t/, /b/, /c/, etc. It is through phonemes that words are distinguished from one another.

Role of Phonological and Phonemic Awareness in Reading Development

Phonological and phonemic awareness do not require written language because phonemic awareness is based entirely upon speech. However, phonological and phonemic awareness are the prerequisites for literacy. Thus, experts recommend that all kindergarten students develop phonemic awareness as part of their reading preparation.

Phonemic Awareness vs. Phonics Skills

Once students are able to recognize phonemes of spoken language, phonics can be implemented in grades K–2. **Phonics** is the direct correspondence between and blending of letters and sounds. Unlike phonemic awareness, phonics requires the presence of print. Phonics often begins with the alphabetic principle, which teaches that letters or other characters represent sounds. Students must be able to identify letters, symbols, and individual sounds before they can blend multiple sounds into word parts and whole words. Thus, phoneme awareness and phonics predict outcomes in word consciousness, vocabulary, reading, and spelling development.

Phonological and Phonemic Awareness Skills

Instruction of phonological awareness includes detecting and identifying word boundaries, onsets/rimes, syllables, and rhyming words. Each of these skills is explained below.

Word boundaries: Students must be able to identify how many letters are in a word and that spaces separate words.

Syllables: A syllable is a unit of speech that contains a vowel sound. A syllable does not necessarily have to be surrounded by consonants. Therefore, every syllable has a rime. However, not every syllable has an onset.

Onset: An onset is the beginning sound of any word. For example, /c/ is the onset in the word cat.

Rime: The **rime** of a word is the sound that follows its onset. The /at/ is the rime in the word cat.

Syllabification: Syllabification is the dividing of words into their component syllables. Syllabification should begin with single-syllable words and progress toward multi-syllable words.

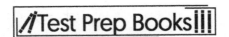

Rhyming words: Rhyming words are often almost identical except for their beginning letter(s). Therefore, rhyming is an effective strategy to implement during the analytic phase of phonics development.

Instruction of phonemic awareness includes recognizing, blending, segmenting, deleting, and substituting phonemes. These skills are explained below:

Phoneme Recognition

Phoneme recognition occurs when students recognize that words are made of separate sounds and they are able to distinguish the initial, middle, and final phonemes within words. Initial awareness of phonemes should be done in isolation and not within words. Then, phoneme awareness can be achieved through shared readings that are supplemented with identification activities, such as the identification of rhyming words.

Blending

Sound blending is the ability to mix together two or more sounds or phonemes. For example, a **consonant blend** is a combination of two or more consonants into a single sound such as /cr/ or /sp/. Blending often begins when the teacher models the slow pronunciation of sound parts within a word. Students are to do likewise, with scaffolding provided by the teacher. Eventually, the pronunciation rate is increased, so that the full word is spoken as it would be in normal conversation.

Segmenting

Sound segmentation is the ability to identify the component phonemes in a word. Segmentation begins with simple, single-syllable words. For instance, a teacher might pronounce the word *tub* and see if students can identify the /t/, /u/, and /b/ sounds. The student must identify all three sounds in order for sound segmentation to be complete.

Deleting

Sound deletion is an oral activity in which one of the phonemes of a spoken word is removed. For example, a teacher may say a word aloud and then ask students to say the word without a specific sound (e.g., "What word would be formed if cat is said without the /c/ sound?"). With repetition, deletion activities can improve phoneme recognition.

Substituting

Like deletion, **substitution** takes place orally and is initiated through modeling. However, instead of deleting a phoneme or syllable, spoken words are manipulated via the substitution of one phoneme for another (e.g., "What word would be formed if we change the /b/ in bun to /r/?").

Promoting Phonological and Phonemic Awareness

The following strategies can be used to develop phonological and phonemic awareness in students that struggle with reading, disabled learners, special-needs students, English Language Learners (ELLs), speakers of nonstandard English, and advanced learners:

> 1. Differentiated instruction for struggling readers, disabled students, or students with special needs should include the re-teaching and/or emphasis of key skills, such as blending and segmenting. Such instruction should be supported through the employment of a variety of concrete examples that explain a concept or task. Teaching strategies of such concepts or tasks

14

should utilize visual, kinesthetic, and tactile modalities, and ample practice time should be allotted.

2. Instruction of phonological and phonemic awareness can also be differentiated for ELLs and speakers of nonstandard English. Most English phonemes are present in other languages. Therefore, teachers can capitalize on the transfer of relevant knowledge, skills, and phonemes from a student's primary language into the English language. In this way, extra attention and instructional emphasis can be applied toward phonemes and phoneme sequences that are nontransferable between the two languages.

3. Advanced learners benefit from phonological and phonemic instruction with greater breadth and depth. Such instruction should occur at a faster pace and expand students' current skills.

Continual Assessment of Phonological and Phonemic Awareness Needs to Occur

Entry-level assessments, progress monitoring, and summative assessments need to be administered in order to determine students' phonological and phonemic awareness. Appropriate formal and informal assessments for such purposes include:

The Yopp-Singer Test of Phonemic Segmentation

The **Yopp-Singer Test of Phonemic Segmentation** is an oral entry-level or summative assessment of phonemic awareness during which a teacher reads twenty-two words aloud one at a time to a single student. The student is to break each word apart by stating the word's sounds in the order that they are heard, and the teacher records the student's responses. Correctly segmented letter sounds are circled and incorrect responses are noted. If a student does well, then he or she is likely to do well in other phonemic areas. Upon poor student performance, the sound(s) with which a student struggles should be emphasized and/or retaught shortly after the time of the assessment.

After the Yopp-Singer Test, the blending of words, syllabification, and/or onset-rime identification should be assessed. The last set of phonological and phonemic skills to be assessed is composed of isolation, blending, deletion, and substitution.

Recognizing Rhyme Assessment

Word awareness, specifically awareness of onset-rime, can be assessed as a progress-monitoring activity. During this assessment, the teacher says two words. Students are to point their thumbs up if the words rhyme and down if the words do not rhyme. Immediate feedback and remediation are provided if the majority of the students respond incorrectly to a word pair.

Isolation or Matching Games

Games can be used to identify initial, medial, and final phonemes. During a phoneme-isolation activity, the teacher says one word at a time. The student is to tell the teacher the first, medial, or last sound of the word. During phoneme-matching activities, a teacher reads a group of words. The student is to say which two words from the group begin or end with the same sound. A similar activity can be completed to assess deletion and/or substitution (e.g., "What word would result if we replaced the /c/ of *cat* with an *h*?"). In this way, teachers can assess if **remediation** or extra instruction on initial, medial, or final phonemes is required and develop lessons accordingly.

Phoneme Blending Assessment

In this assessment, a teacher says all the sounds within a word and a student listens to the teacher and is asked for the word that they hear when the sounds are put together quickly. This skill will be needed

15

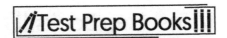

when students learn letter-sound pairs and decipher unknown words in their reading. Thus, mastery of this assessment can be used as an indicator to the teacher that the students are ready to learn higher-level phonological and/or phonemic tasks.

Please note that student results should be recorded, analyzed, and used to determine if students demonstrate mastery over the assessed skill and/or identify the needs of students. If mastery is not demonstrated, then the assessments should be used to determine exactly which letter-sound combinations or other phonemes need to be remediated. Any of the strategies earlier addressed (rhyming, blending, segmenting, deleting, substituting) can be used for such purposes.

Print and the Alphabetic Principle

Print Carries Meaning

Print awareness, the understanding that printed words carry meaning, aids reading development. Print awareness includes the understanding that:

- Words are made of letters, spaces appear between words, and words make sentences.

- Print is organized in a particular way (e.g., read from left to right and top to bottom, read from front to back, etc.), so books must be tracked and held accordingly.

- Different types of print serve specific purposes (magazines, billboards, essays, fiction, etc.).

Print awareness provides the foundation on which all other literacy skills are built. It is often the first stage of reading development. Print awareness helps students develop skills such as word reading, reading comprehension, and letter-sound correspondence. For this reason, a child's performance on tasks relevant to their print awareness is indicative of the child's future reading achievement.

The following strategies can be used to increase print awareness in students:

- An adult reads aloud to students or conducts shared reading experiences. In order to maximize print awareness within the student, the reader should point out the form, function, orientation, and sounds of letters and words.

- Utilize shared reading experiences as a tool for building one-to-one correspondence. **One-to-one correspondence** is the ability to match written letters or words to a spoken word when reading. This can be accomplished by pointing to words as they are read. This helps students make text-to-word connections. Pointing also aids **directionality**, or the ability to track the words that are being read.

- Use the child's environment. To reinforce print awareness, teachers can make a child aware of print in their environment, such as words on traffic signs. Teachers can reinforce this by labeling objects in the classroom.

- Instruct students about book organization during read-alouds. Students should be taught the proper orientation, tracking, and numbering conventions of books. For example, teachers can differentiate the title from the author's name on the front cover of a book.

- Let students practice. Allowing students to practice book-handling skills with wordless books, predictable text, or patterned text will help to instill print awareness.

Relationship Between Spoken and Written Language

Language skills, particularly verbal language skills, are an important precursor to a child's ability to learn to read and improve their reading comprehension. Recognizing and understanding words are key components to spoken and written language. Essentially, both forms of communication are made up of the same elements, including form (phonology, morphology, and syntax), semantics (meaning), pragmatics (what words mean in different situations) and use. Students who have established word skills developed from spoken language enjoy many benefits. Verbal skills inform a student's ability to understand written language, learn vocabulary, recognize letters and sounds, and understand and utilize sentences, particularly those with varied structures. The acquisition of verbal language skills is fundamental to these early reading skills, and it also foster a child's ability to develop, structure, understand, and communicate ideas clearly.

There are several strategies to help foster connections between speaking and writing, and often these include moving between the two in the same activity. One of the first ways to help promote a student's awareness is to work on active listening skills and a student's ability to first hear and recognize a word and then understand its meaning (comprehension skill) in spoken language. In listening, a student then learns to reflect the vocabulary and concepts in their own oral communication. Oral communication here works as the foundation for the same relationships in written language where reading takes on the role of listening and writing takes on the role of speaking. In this way, the relationship between the two modes of communication is established. They mirror one another.

For that reason, it is important to model the same syntax used in writing and speaking. Often, when speaking, we take shortcuts, fail to speak in complete sentences, and use language and structures we would not use when writing. We can and should encourage students to speak the way they would write.

Further, when working with written material, incorporating discussion is invaluable. These exercises may include discussions prior to the reading, such as looking at a title and discussing what students believe the reading will be about, and reading the introduction to identify the type of writing and predict an outcome. After the reading, discussion can and should continue, with references back to the original discussion and the text itself. Regardless of the method, exercises that reinforce the areas of overlap, the understanding of sounds and the letters, letter pairings that recreate those sounds, syntax, and usage are invaluable in raising awareness of the connection between speaking and writing.

Environmental Print in Developing Print Awareness

Environmental print includes the words, letters, and logos we come into contact with in our daily lives, such as household product labels, road signs, advertisements, and clothing labels. Environmental print is the immersive language of everyday life; it is vital to literacy skills and can be a valuable educational tool for early readers as they are able to interact with letters, words, and syntax. It is often the first introduction to reading, even before books. For many students, it also serves as an opportunity to learn new words as well as reinforce reading and comprehension skills in their everyday lives. Further, it reinforces the importance of reading and the autonomy it provides by offering students a practical application of the reading skills they are acquiring in school. Much evidence suggests that interactions with environmental print are a fundamental tool in early literacy. Parents and teachers can bolster this type of learning by asking students to reflect on what they see, seek the letters they see in other

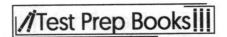
instances of environmental print, or think of other words that incorporate the letters they see or other ways the words might be used.

While environmental print is important at home and in the community, there are plenty of opportunities to include this type of learning in the classroom and foster connections between what students see regularly and what they see in the books they are reading. Classroom environmental strategies can include displaying walls of words, displaying student sentences, and keeping a robust library, especially one that includes students' own work. Assignments can include encouraging students to find vocabulary words in their environment, outside the classroom. Again, the key component here is establishing for the students the connections between using the words in the classroom and encountering them in their daily lives. However, research also suggests that simple exposure to environmental print is beneficial, whether or not there is active engagement and direct instruction related to it. The ability to recognize symbols and logos is an important precursor to early literacy skills. A child's natural curiosity about their environment and desire to understand the context and use of the language they come into daily contact with are often motivating factors.

Book Handling Skills

Feeling comfortable and ready to handle a book is an early indicator that a child is on their way to reading readiness. It is vital for the child to understand that a book contains symbols, the symbols have meaning, and the meaning is accessible to them. Book handling skills suggest an understanding of those concepts, and they include the ability to hold a book properly, open it, and turn the pages.

The first step to introducing book handling skills is to have a book-abundant environment. By developing familiarity and establishing books as an everyday object to be held and explored, educators and parents can take the first steps in building comfort with handling books. This means that books should be provided in nearly every environment a child spends time in, whether that be in the car (or in transport to school or daycare), at home, and in daycare or school.

In early stages, include books made of durable materials as they may be seen as toys. This will encourage toddlers to play with the books, hold them, open them, and mirror any "reading" they may see. At home and in the classroom, child-accessible libraries and book corners should be created so that children are free to explore on their own. A good amount of book handling skills will be developed in joint reading activities with adults, but access creates the freedom to feel a sense of ownership over books.

Additionally, parents and educators should create opportunities for children to see what happens with a book. When adults read with children, it's key for the child to see the page, see the words, and observe the behaviors associated with the book such as turning the pages. As early as possible, adult readers should start identifying parts of the book by pointing as each is read, such as the title, the author, and perhaps a dedication. They should explain to the child what this information says about the book itself.

When a child is ready, let them begin to turn pages in the book. Pointing to both pictures and words in the book and discussing with a child while reading helps attach significance to the words and information in the book, all while developing early reading skills. This activity can then be extended beyond books and into the child's everyday environment to continue to build familiarity with language and reading. Creating environmental print in home and classroom can be quite beneficial. It's helpful to label items at home and in the classroom, and then point out the items as they are identified.

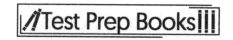

Finally, making books with stapled blank pages can encourage children to create their own books and fill the pages, interacting with book and text.

Directionality of Print

Directionality of print refers to a student's understanding that, when reading a book, there are keys to how readers move through the physical book itself as well as a specific pattern (direction) to reading the text. Moving through a book, readers start at the front, and then, on each page, begin at the top and move to the bottom of the page. Each individual page is read left to right, as are the words on the page itself. Teachers will need to demonstrate, with a pointer, how a reader's eyes then sweep to the start of the next line. Pages are then turned left to right as well. Because this pattern of movement is not natural, students must learn to focus on tracking print.

Early on, strategies can include discussions and activities that focus on identifying the title of a book or the summary on the back of the book to establish how the book is used to access content. Once inside the book, labeling where a student starts reading with a sticker or an identifiable mark can be very helpful. Similarly, classroom space and a student's personal space can be marked with labels to help students identify and remember left and right as a technique to remember where to start reading.

Further, when working with stories and books students are reading, have students identify the first and last word in a sentence. This also provides an opportunity to learn about capitalization. Moving from first to last word and tracing that path with a finger is also a strategy that adults can model, as it visually demonstrates the path that a reader's eye takes.

Class activities can include discussions about where to start reading in a book and manipulating words to mirror sentences with a focus on identifying the first and last word. Again, the goal with these strategies is repetition, so that following the directionality of print becomes habit for a student as their reading skills improve.

Tracking Print in Connected Text

Learning to track print in connected text is a vital skill in improving reading. While students may be able to identify and read individual words, the key to becoming a strong and confident reader is the ability to read and understand connected text, or sentences. In order to develop this skill, students must be able to quickly find and identify words in sentences as well as follow along with the direction of text (left to right) while reading or while following along with a reader.

In order to work on building these skills, reading aloud while students have a copy of the text available to them is a great strategy. Projecting the words onto a whiteboard or classroom space is another great activity. Enlarging print by projecting words mimics early experiences of reading with adults and is familiar and engaging to students. Additionally, instruction here should include attention to spacing, capitalization, and commonly used or paired words and phrases. To move beyond this, having students use the pointer to follow along builds on the skill.

At first, start with texts students are familiar with to build confidence and create a foundation of familiar words before introducing new texts. To start this process, instruction should begin with modeled reading, followed by having students read along with the teacher, then having students read as a group after the teacher reads a line, and finally having the students read a line each, independently.

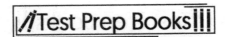

Once this strategy is employed, it can be broken down even further by incorporating similar strategies with familiar and repeated texts, songs, rhymes, or poems. By creating individual word cards, students can reconstruct the sentences of those songs, rhymes, or poems by recalling the structure of the phrases and sentences themselves.

As students begin to read independently, provide them with a pointer, ruler, or card to allow them to isolate single lines of text and track the words as they read. By placing this tracking tool above a line of text, students can then also practice the sweep of the eye that naturally moves to the next line.

Strategies to Develop Letter Recognition

Among the skills that are used to determine reading readiness, letter identification is the strongest predictor. **Letter recognition** is the identification of each letter in the alphabet. Letter recognition does not include letter-sound correspondences; however, learning about and being able to recognize letters may increase student motivation to learn letter sounds. Also, the names of many letters are similar to their sounds, so letter recognition serves as a gateway for the letter-sound relationships that are needed for reading to occur. Similarly, the ability to differentiate between uppercase and lowercase letters is beneficial in determining where a sentence begins and ends.

To be fluent in letter identification, students should be able to identify letter names in and out of context with automaticity. In order to obtain such familiarity with the identification of letters, students need ample experience, acquaintance, and practice with letters. Explicit instruction in letter recognition, practice printing uppercase and lowercase letters of the alphabet, and consistent exposure to printed letters are essential in the instruction of letter recognition.

Research has revealed that the following sequencing guidelines are necessary to effectively promote letter naming and identification:

1. The initial stage includes visual discrimination of shapes and curved lines.

2. Once students are able to identify and discriminate shapes with ease, then letter formations can be introduced. During the introduction of letter shapes, two letters that share visual (*p* and *q*) or auditory (/a/ and /u/) similarities should never be presented in back-to-back.

3. Next, uppercase letters are introduced. Uppercase letters are introduced before lowercase letters because they are easier to discriminate visually than lowercase letters. When letter formations are first presented to a student, their visual system analyzes the vertical, horizontal, and curved orientations of the letters. Therefore, teachers should use think-alouds when instructing how to write the shape of each letter. During think-alouds, teachers verbalize their own thought processes that occur when writing each part of a given letter. Students should be encouraged to do likewise when practicing printing the letters.

4. Once uppercase letters are mastered, lowercase letters can be introduced. High-frequency lowercase letters (*a, e, t*) are introduced prior to low-frequency lowercase letters (*q, x, z*).

5. Once the recognition of letters is mastered, students need ample time manipulating and utilizing the letters. This can be done through sorting, matching, comparing, and writing activities.

20

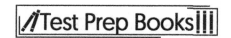

Letter Formation

Most children are very eager to pick up pen and paper, particularly when that behavior is modeled by the adults in their lives. However, the expectation that writing will come naturally from a child merely playing at writing is misplaced. Failure to teach proper handwriting skills may result in struggles elsewhere in the writing process, so it's key to include letter formation lessons in the classroom.

Prior to beginning any work on letter formation, educators should ensure that students have a firm grasp on shapes such as squares, circles, triangles, and lines, as well as patterns that combine them. Students should be able to create and copy basic shapes and patterns. In order to practice this, tracing is a great activity until students can recreate items on their own. Shapes and patterns can mimic the same movements and shapes found in letter writing, and so tracing prepares the student for the next step.

When starting to teach letter formation, again, tracing is a good tactic. Instructing students on where to start tracing and which path to follow is also fundamental to their success later on. For this reason, instruction working with letters that have similar shapes or patterns is recommended. These include letters like *b, d,* and *p,* which all include a circle and a line. Once a student has become confident in tracing, the next step is to have them copy letters. They still have a guide in front of them and can work from that. Once they have become comfortable with that exercise, have students write the letters on their own. Even as they do this independently, it may be beneficial to provide a starting point and other touch points to work on size and correct shape.

Additionally, other classroom activities can be used to reinforce the shapes and formation of letters. Students can participate in games in which, with classmates, they line themselves up in the shape of a letter or where they must make the shape of the letter by hopping along a path. Finally, every student loves to learn to write their name, so that's always a great place to start with any of these activities, as it creates immediate investment and interest.

Alphabetic Principle

The **alphabetic principle** is the understanding of the names and sounds produced by letters, letter patterns, and symbols printed on a page. Through the alphabetic principle, students learn letter-sound correspondence, phonemic awareness, and the application of simple decoding skills such as the sounding out and blending of letter sounds. Since reading is essentially the blending together of multiple letter sounds, the alphabetic principle is crucial in reading development.

As with the instruction of letter recognition, research has revealed the following sequence to be effective in the teaching of the alphabetic principle:

> Letter-sound relationships need to be taught explicitly and in isolation. The rate at which new letter-sound correspondences can be presented will be unique to the student group. The order in which letters are presented should permit students to read words quickly. Therefore, letter-sound pairs that are used frequently should be presented before letter-sound pairs with lower utility. Similarly, letter-sound pairs that can be pronounced in isolation without distortion (f, m, s, r) should be presented first. Instruction of letters that sound similar should not be presented in proximity.

> Once single-letter and sound combinations are mastered, consonant blends and clusters (*br, cr, gr*) can be presented.

21

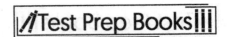

Teaching Letter-Sound Correspondence

When children begin to learn the various letter-sound correspondences, their phonemic awareness begins to overlap with their awareness of orthography and reading. One of the widely accepted strategies to employ when introducing children to letter-sound correspondences is to begin with those correspondences that occur the most frequently in simple English words. In an effort to help build confidence in young learners, educators are encouraged to introduce only a few letter-sound combinations at a time and provide ample opportunities for practice and review before introducing new combinations. Although there is no formally established order for the introduction of letter-sound correspondences, educators are encouraged to consider the following general guidelines. However, they should also keep in mind the needs, experiences, and current literacy levels of the students. The following is intended as a general guide only:

1. a	6. n	11. g	16. l	21. x
2. m	7. c	12. h	17. e	22. v
3. t	8. d	13. i	18. r	23. y
4. p	9. u	14. f	19. w	24. z
5. o	10. s	15. b	20. k	25. j
				26. q

As a generally accepted rule, short vowels should be introduced ahead of long vowels, and uppercase letters should be mastered before the introduction of their lowercase counterparts, although there are some arguments for introducing lowercase letters first or introducing both uppercase and lowercase letters together.

Spelling conventions in the English language are primarily concerned with three areas: mechanics, usage, and sentence formation.

Mechanics

For primary students who are just beginning to master the alphabetic principle, educators should first concentrate on proper letter formation, the spelling of high-frequency words and sight words, and offering classroom discussions to promote the sharing of ideas. When children begin to write in sentences to share their thoughts and feelings in print, educators may consider the introduction of an author's chair, in which students read their writing out loud to their classmates.

Although the phonetic spelling or invented spelling that primary students employ in these early stages may not be the conventional spelling of certain words, it allows primary students to practice the art and flow of writing. It works to build their confidence in the writing process. This is not the time for educators to correct spelling, punctuation, or capitalization errors, as young learners may quickly lose interest in writing and may lose self-confidence.

One strategy to employ early on to help students with proper spelling is to ensure there is an easily accessible and updated word wall that employs high-frequency words and sight words. Students should be encouraged to refer to the word wall while they write.

Usage

Usage concerns itself with word order, verb tense, and subject-verb agreement among other areas. As primary children often have a basic knowledge of how to use oral language effectively in order to

22

communicate, this area of spelling conventions may require less initial attention than the mechanics of spelling. During read-aloud and shared reading activities, educators may wish to point out punctuation marks found in print, model how to read these punctuation marks, and periodically discuss their importance in the reading and writing process.

When children begin to engage in writing exercises, educators may wish to prompt self-editing skills by asking if each sentence begins with a capital and ends with a period, question mark, or exclamation point.

Sentence Formation

Verbs, nouns, adverbs, and adjectives all play significant roles in the writing process. However, for primary students, these concepts are fairly complex to understand. One instruction approach that may prove effective is to categorize a number of simple verbs, nouns, adverbs, and adjectives on index cards by color coordination. Educators can then ask one child to choose a noun card and another student to choose a verb card. The children can then face the class and read their words starting with the noun and then the verb. The students can even try reading the verb first followed by the noun. A class discussion can follow, analyzing whether or not the sentences made sense and what words might need to be added to give the sentence more meaning.

Developing Print Awareness, Letter Recognition, and the Alphabetic Principle

The following strategies to develop print awareness, letter recognition, and the alphabetic principle within students who struggle with reading, disabled and special-needs students, English Learners, speakers of nonstandard English, and advanced learners have been identified:

Streamlining the skills and concepts presented and reducing the pace of instruction is essential in the development of print awareness, letter recognition, and the alphabetic principle of struggling readers and students with disabilities or special needs. Assessments can be used to determine the letters and sounds with which each student struggles. These letters and sounds should be the focus of instruction. Key skills and concepts need to be supported with a variety of concrete examples and activities that utilize auditory, kinesthetic, and tactile modalities. Extended practice and re-teaching of concepts are beneficial.

When working with ELLs or speakers of nonstandard English, teachers should capitalize on the transfer of relevant print awareness, letter recognition, and alphabetic principle concepts from the students' primary languages to the English language. However, not all languages are alphabetic. Also, key features of alphabets vary, including letters, directionality, and phonetic regularity. Therefore, teachers may need to employ the direct and explicit strategies presented above with ELLs, regardless of age.

Instruction that occurs at a faster pace, with greater breadth and depth, will benefit the development of print awareness, letter recognition, and the alphabetic principle in advanced learners.

Role of Phonics in Promoting Reading Development

Strategies for Teaching Phonics

Phonics incorporates the alphabetic principle and decoding strategies. Phonics knowledge includes recognizing letter-sound correspondence. Students use phonics to sound out letter sequences and blend the sounds of the letter sequences together in order to form words.

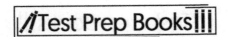
Phonics instruction should begin with the decoding of simple syllable patterns, such as *am* and *map*. Upon mastery of simple patterns, more complex patterns can be introduced, such as *tape* or *spot*. The following characteristics are present in an effective phonics program:

- The goal and purpose are clarified at the beginning of each lesson.

- Visual and concrete material, such as letter cards and dry-erase boards, are used.

- Direct instruction of letter sounds is provided through a series of mini lessons.

- Direct instruction in the decoding of letter sounds found in words is provided, such as sounding out letters and blending sounds into words.

Students partake in guided and independent practice during which immediate feedback is provided. Activities such as word reading and word sorts, which incorporate previously taught spelling patterns, can reinforce explicit phonics instruction.

Effective phonics programs allow students to apply new phonics skills in a broad range of reading and writing contexts.

Proper Sequencing of Complex Linguistic Units

Research has shown that phonics and sight-word instruction is best accomplished using the following steps:

1. Phonics instruction should begin with **consonant sounds**. Consonant sounds block the flow of air through the mouth. Consonants can form either continuous or stop sounds. **Continuous sounds** are those that can be said for a long period of time, such as /mmm/. **Stop sounds** are said in short bursts, such as /t/.

2. Teach the following common and regular letter combinations:

   a. **Consonant digraphs:** Consonant digraphs are combinations of two or three consonants that work together to make a single sound. Examples of consonant digraphs are *sh, ch*, and *th*.

   b. **Consonant blends:** Consonant blends are sometimes referred to as **consonant clusters**. Consonant blends occur when two or three consonant sounds are blended together to make a single consonant sound. Unlike consonant digraphs, each letter in a consonant blend is identifiable. Examples of consonant blends are *gl, gr, pl, sm*, and *sp*.

   c. **Vowel digraphs:** Vowel digraphs are sets of two vowels that spell a single sound. Examples of vowel digraph pairs are *ow, ie, ae, ou, ei, ie*, and *oo*.

   d. **Diphthongs:** Diphthongs are the sounds created by letter/vowel combinations. Examples of diphthongs are *ow* as in town or cow and *igh* as in high or tight.

   e. **R- and l- controlled vowels:** These are words in which a vowel sound is controlled by an r, l, or ll following it. Examples include *car, girl, old*, or *call*.

24

3. Teach common **inflected morphological units**, which include word parts such as affixes or root words. Examples of morphological units that could be presented at this time are suffixes such as *-ed, -er, -est, -ing,* and *-s.*

4. Present common word patterns of increasing difficulty. **Word patterns** are made of sequences (or patterns) of vowels (V) and consonants (C). Examples include VC (*ear, egg, eat,* etc.), CVC (*cat, bat, map,* etc.), CCVC (*stop, frog, spot,* etc.), CVVC (*head, lead, dead,* etc.), CVCe (*same, make, pale,* etc.), etc.

5. Teach identification of **vowel-consonant patterns** and **multisyllabic-word syllabication**.

6. Discuss why some words are irregular, meaning that they are not decodable. Students may struggle decoding some words because the sounds of the letters found within the words do not follow predictable phonics patterns.

7. Time should be allotted for the instruction of common irregular sight words that are not readily decodable. However, this is usually not done until students are able to decode words that follow predictable phonic patterns at a rate of one letter-sound per second. Irregular sight words need to be gradually introduced. Words that are visually similar should not be shown in proximity to one another. The irregular words need to be practiced until students can read them with automaticity. New words are not introduced until the previous sets are mastered. The words are continuously reintroduced and reviewed thereafter.

8. When students first begin reading, they may be able to decode some words that have not yet been introduced to them merely by using letter-sound correspondences. The instruction of irregular words should be applied to these words as well.

Role of Phonics in Developing Rapid, Automatic Word Recognition

Word recognition occurs when students are able to recognize and read a word automatically and correctly. Phonics and sight word instruction help with the promotion of accurate and automatic word identification and recognition. Once students are able to readily identify and recognize words, then they can focus on the meaning of the text and development of reading comprehension skills.

Phonics instruction stresses letter-sound correspondences and the manipulation of phonemes. Through phonics instruction, students discover the different sounds of a spoken language and how a written language's letters and symbols relate to one another. It is through the application of phonics principles that students are able to decode words. When a word is decoded, the letters that make up the printed word are translated into sounds. When students are able to recognize and manipulate letter-sound relationships of single-syllable words, then they are able to apply such relationships to decode more complex words. In this way, phonics aids reading fluency and reading comprehension.

Sight words, sometimes referred to as high-frequency words, are words that are used often but may not follow the regular principles of phonics. Sight words may also be defined as words that students are able to readily recognize and read without having to sound them out. Students are encouraged to memorize words by sight so their reading fluency is not deterred through the frequent decoding of regularly-occurring irregular words. In this way, sight word recognition aids reading fluency and reading comprehension.

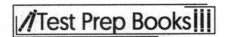
Role of Automaticity in Developing Reading Fluency

Automaticity is a student's ability to quickly recognize familiar words and read them. However, the ability to do this does not create a fluent reader, which is defined as one who reads with expression. Automaticity does not equal fluency. In fact, the ability to recognize words simply means they can be read quickly and individually, but not necessarily in the phrases or sections that connect them to other words and attribute meaning to them.

Automaticity is the first step in developing fluency, though. Fluency involves a student's ability to read with speed, accuracy, and appropriate expression. Obviously, a student must be able to read words easily and quickly to be able to move into the next stages of reading, and for that reason, fluency comes with familiarity.

To develop skills in fluency, it is best to start with a text that the student is familiar with and is at their reading level. Students are then able to focus more on building reading speed and understanding meaning than on learning individual words or sounding them out.

A popular method for improving fluency relies fairly heavily on automaticity in that it asks students to read the same passage repeatedly. First, the passage is read, fluently, by the teacher, and then the student is asked to read the passage. Not only does the student read the same passage, but they do so aloud to receive feedback while reading. Teachers can correct pronunciation and address issues related to phonemic awareness. Additionally, playing recordings of fluent readers reading the passage or pairing students with more fluent readers may work. Again, the idea here is that automaticity is gained through multiple readings of a passage, and the student can then move on to reading fluently.

There is currently no research that fully supports independent reading as a viable strategy to build fluency based on automaticity. Automaticity and fluency are developed the more a student reads; therefore, silent reading may also help develop both skills.

Strategies to Help Read New and/or Difficult Words

Children who are developing reading fluency and comprehension skills can become frustrated when presented with unfamiliar words in a given text. With direct phonics instruction, educators can teach children to decode words and then use context clues to define the words while reading. If children have a strong enough understanding of language structures, educators can ask them to consider what part of speech the unknown word might be and use that information to help infer its meaning. Focusing on visual clues, such as drawings and photographs, may help children decipher unknown words. They could also look for the word in another section of the text to see how it relates to the overall meaning. Competent readers **self-monitor**, meaning they listen to themselves as they read both to notice any discrepancies between the words they see and the sounds they say and to ensure that what they have read makes sense.

One of the most valuable strategies for helping children to understand new words in their reading is **pre-teaching**, in which teachers select the unfamiliar words in the text and introduce them to the class before reading. Educators using this method should be careful not to simply ask the children to read the text and then spell the new words correctly. They should also provide clear definitions and give the children the opportunity to read these words in various sentences to decipher word meaning. This method can dramatically reduce how often children stop reading in order to reflect on unknown words. Educators are often unsure as to whether to correct every mispronounced word a child makes when reading. If the mispronounced word still makes sense, it is sometimes better to allow the child to

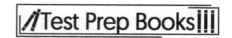

continue to read, since the more the child stops, the more the child's reading comprehension and fluency are negatively affected.

Stages of Spelling Development

Spelling development occurs in stages. In order, these stages are the pre-phonetic stage, the semiphonetic stage, the phonetic stage, the transitional stage, and the conventional stage. Each stage is explained below. Ways in which phonics and vocabulary development fit into the spelling stages are discussed. Instructional strategies for each phase of spelling are suggested.

Spelling development begins with the **pre-phonetic stage**, which is marked by an incomplete understanding of the alphabetic principle and letter-sound correspondences. During this stage, students participate in pre-communicative writing, which appears to be a jumble of letter-like forms rather than a series of discrete letters. Students' precommunicative writing samples can be used as informal assessments of their understanding of the alphabetic principle and knowledge of letter-sound correspondences.

Pre-phonetic stage of spelling development

The pre-phonetic stage is followed by the **semiphonetic stage**, in which students understand that letters represent sounds. The alphabetic principle may be understood, but letter recognition may not yet be fully developed. In this stage, single letters may be used to represent entire words (e.g., *U* for *you*). Other times, multiple syllables within words may be omitted. Writing produced by students in this stage

27

is still virtually unreadable. Teachers may ask students to provide drawings to supplement their writing to better determine what a student intended to write.

Semiphonetc stage of writing

IEETDNTJ

I eat donuts.

The third stage in spelling development is the **phonetic stage**. In this stage, students have mastered letter-sound correspondences. Although letters may be written backward or upside down, phonetic spellers are able to write all of the letters in the alphabet. Because phonetic spellers have limited sight vocabulary, they will often spell irregular words incorrectly; however, these incorrectly spelled words may phonetically sound like the spoken word. Additionally, student writing becomes systematic. For example, students are likely to use one letter to represent a digraph or letter blend (e.g., ƒ for /ph/).

Phonetic stage of writing

I am FIDIN BIRDS.

Spelling instruction of common consonant patterns, short vowel sounds, and common affixes or rimes can begin during the phonetic stage. Thus, spelling instruction during the phonetic stage coincides with the instruction of phonics and phonemic awareness that also occurs during this stage of development.

28

Word walls are advantageous during the phonetic stage because they provide visual groupings of words that share common consonant-vowel patterns or letter clusters. Students are encouraged to add words to each group. As a result, word walls promote strategic spelling, vocabulary development, common letter combinations, and common morphological units.

The **transitional stage** of spelling occurs when a student has developed a small sight vocabulary and a solid understanding of letter-sound correspondences. Thus, spelling dependence on phonology decreases. Instead, dependence on visual representation and word structure increases. As sight word vocabulary increases during the transition stage, the correct spelling of irregular words will also increase. However, students may still struggle to spell words with long vowel sounds.

Transitional stage of spelling

Differentiation of spelling instruction often begins during the transitional stage. Instruction ought to be guided by data collected through informal observations and assessments. Depending on individual needs, lessons may include sight word recognition, morphology, etymology, reading, and writing. Students can begin learning about homophones during the transitional stage. **Homophones** are words that sound the same but have different spellings and meanings (e.g., *their* and *there*). Additionally, students should be expected to begin writing full sentences at the transitional stage. Writing reinforces phonics, vocabulary, and correct spelling of words.

The **conventional stage** comes last, occurring after a student's sight word vocabulary is well developed and the student is able to read fluently with comprehension. By this stage, students know the basic rules of phonics. They are able to deal with consonants, multiple vowel-consonant blends, homophones,

digraphs, and irregular spellings. Due to an increase in sight word recognition at this stage, a conventional speller is able to recognize when a word is spelled incorrectly.

Conventional stage

It is at the conventional spelling stage that spelling instruction can begin to focus on content-specific vocabulary words and words with unusual spellings. In order to further reinforce vocabulary development of such content-specific words and apply phonic skills, students should be encouraged to use the correct spelling of such words within various writing activities.

For even the best conventional spellers, some words will still cause consistent trouble. Students can keep track of words that they consistently spell incorrectly or find confusing in word banks so they can isolate and eventually eliminate their individualized errors. Students can use their word banks as references when they come across a word with which they struggle. Students may also spend time consciously committing the words in their banks to memory through verbal or written practice.

Letter-Sound Correspondence and Beginning Decoding

The ability to break apart a word into its individual phonemes is referred to as **segmenting**. Segmenting words can greatly aid in a child's ability to recognize, read, and spell an entire word. In literacy instruction, **blending** is when the reader connects segmented parts to create an entire word. Segmenting and blending practice work together like pieces of a puzzle to help children practice newly-acquired vocabulary. Educators can approach segmenting and blending using a multi-sensory approach. For example, a child can manipulate letter blocks to build words and pull them apart. An educator may even ask the child to listen to the word being said and ask him or her to find the letter blocks that build each phoneme, one at a time:

/m/ /u/ /g/

/b/ /a/ /t/

30

/r/ /u/ /n/

Once children are able to blend and segment phonemes, they are ready for the more complex skill of blending and segmenting syllables, onsets, and rimes. Using the same multi-sensory approach, children may practice blending the syllables of familiar words on a word wall, using letter blocks, paper and pencil, or sounding them out loud. Once they blend the words together, students can then practice segmenting those same words, studying their individual syllables, letters, and sounds. Educators may again read a word out loud and ask children to write or build the first syllable, followed by the next, and so on. The very same practice can be used to identify the onset. Children can work on writing and/or building this sound followed by the word's rime. Word families and rhyming words are ideal for this type of exercise so that children can more readily see the parts of each word. Using words that rhyme can turn this exercise into a fun and engaging activity.

Once children have demonstrated the ability to independently blend and segment phonemes, syllables, onsets, and rimes, educators may present a more challenging exercise that involves substitutions and deletions. As these are more complex skills, children will likely benefit from repeated practice and modeling. Using word families and words that rhyme when teaching this skill will make the activity more enjoyable, and it will also greatly aid in a child's overall comprehension.

Substitution and Deletion Using Onset and Rime				
Word	**Onset Deletion**	**Rime Deletion**	**Onset Substitution**	**Rime Substitution**
Run	un	r	Fun	rat
Bun	un	b	Gun	bat
Sun	un	s	Nun	sat

Substitution and Deletion Using Phonemes		
Word	Phoneme substitution	Phoneme Deletion
Sit	sat	si
Bit	bat	bi
Hit	hat	hi

31

Substitution and Deletion Using Syllables

Word	Syllable Substitution	Syllable Deletion
cement	lament or, cedar	ce
moment	statement, or motive	mo
basement	movement, or baseball	base

Decoding Single-Syllable Words

While reading has much to do with conceptual knowledge of English and awareness of the structures and rules of the language, recognizing word patterns can also help students see basic English principles. Being able to recognize familiar word patterns essentially helps students decode the pronunciation and even the meaning of unfamiliar words by recognizing core linguistic components.

The first step in identifying patterns is knowing how to sort words. When describing and searching for word patterns, sound is key. To begin, instructors can have students (or themselves) list single-syllable words that share similar beginnings, endings, and vowel sounds. Examining **affixes** (the letters before or after the root word), which change a word's initial meaning, is also key. For example, students can recognize that the *a* sound used in *bat* and *cat* is the same. Recognizing this sorting method provides insight on how to pronounce the words *that* or *fat*. Thus, students gain a tool for decoding words they haven't seen before.

Teachers should also examine words that are spelled differently but sound the same. For example, *veer*, *near*, and *tier* share a sound pattern but are spelled differently. This sheds light on how the vowels *ee*, *ea*, and *ie* sound between consonants. For an activity, students can group vowel combinations into columns that indicate a shared sound to help them recognize the connection between sound and spelling patterns. Another engaging activity would be to have students create small poems that use words with a specific sound. For example, using the vowel *i*, students can be encouraged to create a rhyme with three words, each with one syllable. The results should share common vowel and consonant sounds, such as *tip*, *ship*, and *dip* or *fig*, *lip*, and *skid*. Note how the vowel remains constant even while the consonants change.

Some single-syllable words, such as common sight words, have no clear pattern. The best way to teach these words (*the*, *to*, and others) is to have students visualize and learn them just as they are. One easy activity would be to play bingo or a similar visual game using single-syllable sight words to build familiarity with the everyday terms.

Use of Phonics Generalizations to Decode Words in Connected Text

The methodology of grouping and recognizing patterns in single-syllable words can also apply to multisyllable words. However, because these words are more complex, the pattern scope must be broader. Teachers must reexamine similar-sounding vowel groups and consonant relationships as with

singular-syllable words. It may also help to review the six syllable spelling patterns: open, closed, vowel team, silent vowel *e*, consonant *le*, and *r*-controlled patterns.

As a class activity, students can spend time grouping individual words into the spelling formats to demonstrate their knowledge of English sounds and how the letters function in the words. The instructor should explain the categories, then name a word, have the students say it back, and finally group the word into its appropriate category. For example, the word *throat* has a kind of *oh* sound because of the vowel team *oa*. Instructors should also distinguish closed- and open-syllable spelling patterns. **Open** reflects a long vowel ending sound, such as *tiger,* with an exaggerated *-er* sounding ending; alternately, the **closed** pattern reflects a short vowel sound toward the end as seen in the word *darken*.

The **r-controlled vowels** are also important to highlight. Words such as *fur* and *car* stand out because of how the *r* sounds more prevalent than the vowel. To practice this, students can list words such as *cart, short, turtle,* and *fertile* on the board so they can have a visual reference, or the teacher can go around the class and have students name such words aloud. Again, it's important to hear the words and examine them visually in order for students to grasp how the words function and operate.

With multisyllable words, it's important to review consonant diagraphs and how they function. Because there are many diagraphs with different pronunciations, it's important to demonstrate how they differ in various words, such as the *ch* in *Christmas* and *charity*. Students should also be able to compare how moving diagraphs within words alters pronunciations, such as with *anchor* or *pitch,* respectively.

When it comes to approaching multisyllable words in general, teachers should emphasize sounding out the words in order to grasp the pronunciation. Another good strategy for learning larger words is to have students break a word down by syllables and then combine them to complete the whole word. Again, an interactive approach to these principles will help students grasp the material more easily.

Semantic and Syntactic Clues

Reading competence of multisyllabic words is accomplished through phonics skills that are accompanied by a reader's ability to recognize morphological structures within words. **Structural analysis** is a word recognition skill that focuses on the meaning of word parts, or morphemes, during the introduction of a new word. Therefore, the instruction of structural analysis focuses on the recognition and application of morphemes. **Morphemes** are word parts such as base words, prefixes, inflections, and suffixes. Students can use structural analysis skills to find familiar word parts within an unfamiliar word in order to decode the word and determine the definition of the new word. Identification and association of such word segments also aids the proper pronunciation and spelling of new multisyllabic words.

Similarly, learning to use phonics skills with more difficult words depends on a reader's ability to notice syllable structures within words that have more than one syllable. **Syllabic analysis**, or **syllabication**, is a skill that teaches students how to analyze words and separate them into syllables. **Syllables** are phonological units that contain a vowel sound. Teaching students how to break apart multisyllabic words into morphological and phonological units can greatly help them not to be intimidated by long words, since these tools will help them use syllable types to make longer words seem like a series of smaller words. The identified syllables can then be blended, pronounced, and/or written together as a single word. This helps students learn to decode and encode the longer words more accurately and efficiently with less anxiety. Thus, syllabic analysis leads to the rapid word recognition that is critical in reading fluency and comprehension.

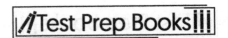

The following table identifies the six basic syllable patterns that should be explicitly taught during syllabic instruction:

Basic Syllable Patterns		
Name of Syllable Type	Characteristics of Syllable Type	Examples
Closed	A syllable with a single vowel closed in by a consonant.	lab, bog, an
Open	A syllable that ends with a single vowel. Note that the letter *y* acts as a vowel.	go, me, sly
Vowel-Consonant-Silent *e*	A syllable with a single vowel followed by a consonant then *e*.	like, rake, note, obese
Vowel Teams	A syllable that has two consecutive vowels. Note that the letters *w* and *y* act as vowels.	meat, pertain, bay, toad, window
R-controlled	A syllable with one or two vowels followed by the letter *r*.	car, jar, fir, sir, collar, turmoil
Consonant *le (-al, -el)* Also called final stable	A syllable that has a consonant followed by the letters *le*, *al*, or *el*.	puddle, stable, uncle, bridal, pedal
Other final stable syllables	A syllable at the end of words can be taught as a recognizable unit such as *cious, age, ture, tion*, or *sion*.	pension, elation, puncture, stumpage, fictitious

Decoding and Encoding

Decoding and encoding are **reciprocal phonological skills**, meaning that their steps are opposite of each other.

Decoding is the application of letter-sound correspondences, letter patterns, and other phonics relationships that help students read and correctly pronounce words. Decoding helps students to recognize and read words quickly, increasing reading fluency and comprehension. The steps of the decoding process are as follows:

1. The student identifies a written letter or letter combination.

2. The student identifies the sound of that letter or letter combination.

3. The student understands how the word's different letters or letter combinations fit together.

4. The student verbally blends the letter and letter combinations together to form a word.

Encoding is the spelling of words. In order to properly spell words, students must be familiar with letter/sound correspondences. Students must be able to put together phonemes, digraphs or blends, morphological units, consonant/vowel patterns, etc. The steps of encoding are identified below:

1. The student understands that letters and sounds make up words.

2. The student segments the sound parts of a word.

3. The student identifies the letter or letter combinations that correspond to each sound part.

4. The student then writes the letters and letter combinations in order to create the word.

Because the stages of decoding and encoding are reciprocal skills, phonics knowledge supports the development of reading and spelling. Likewise, the development of spelling skills reinforces phonics and decoding. In fact, the foundation of all good spelling programs is alignment with reading instruction and students' reading levels. Phonics instruction begins with simple syllable patterns and then progresses toward more complex patterns, the sounds of morphemes, and strategies for decoding multisyllabic words. Through this process, new vocabulary is developed. Sight word instruction should not begin until students are able to decode target words with automaticity and accuracy. Spelling is the last instructional component to be introduced.

Promoting Automaticity and Fluency

Several factors influence a student's reading development skills. Students learn to read at varying ages. A student's background knowledge, first language acquisition, and family involvement in reading all affect a student's progress. Therefore, when to introduce fluency instruction cannot be determined merely by a student's age or grade level. Fluency instruction begins when a student can use basic decoding skills and can read 90% of connected text with accuracy. Routinely assessing a student's decoding and accuracy skills will help determine when to begin fluency instruction.

Even if students do not yet display automaticity, modeling can be used as an initial introduction to fluency. Modeling demonstrates social norms of reading rate and prosody while building vocabulary, academic language, and background knowledge.

Practice, Guidance, and Feedback

Accuracy and reading rate are fundamental components of fluency, but it's important to remember that practice is an essential component of effective fluency instruction. When teachers provide daily opportunities for students to learn words and utilize word-analysis skills, accuracy and rate are likely to increase.

Oral reading accompanied by guidance and feedback from teachers, peers, and/or parents has been shown to improve fluency significantly. In order to be beneficial, such feedback needs to provide targeted and differentiated advice on areas where a student needs improvement. It's also recommended that teachers provide feedback that includes a variety of strategies.

Research-Based, Systematic, Explicit Strategies That Improve Fluency and Accuracy

Word-reading accuracy requires that students have a strong understanding of letter-sound correspondence and the ability to blend the sounds together accurately. Providing systematic, explicit instruction in phonemic awareness, phonics, and decoding skills will cultivate such accuracy. When

students are readily able to identify high-frequency sight words, their accuracy improves. Therefore, instructors should provide ample opportunities to practice these words.

Research-Based, Systematic, Explicit Strategies That Improve Fluency and Reading Rate

Reading aloud has proven effective in strengthening reading fluency. Whisper-reading accompanied by teacher monitoring has also proven effective for students who don't yet display automaticity in their decoding skills. Timed reading of sight phrases or stories also improves fluency with respect to rate. During a **timed-reading** exercise, the number of words read in a given amount of time is recorded. Routinely administering timed readings and displaying the results in graphs and charts has been shown to increase student motivation.

Timed-repeated readings, where a student reads and re-reads familiar texts in a given time, is a commonly used instructional strategy to increase reading speed, accuracy, and comprehension. Students read and re-read the passage until they reach their target rate.

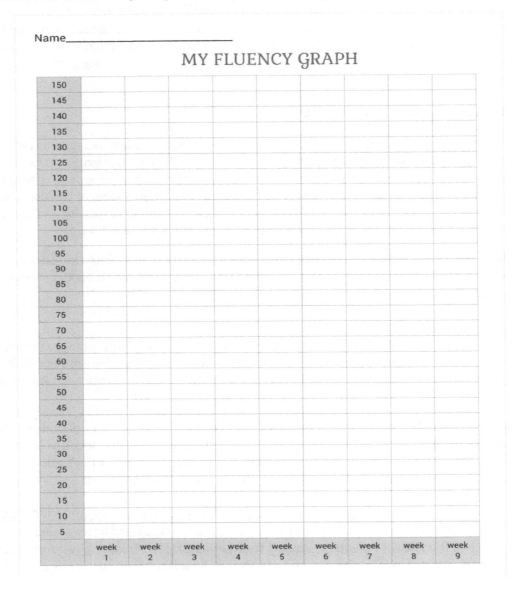

Research-Based, Systematic, Explicit Strategies That Improve Fluency and Prosody

Reading aloud not only improves the rate but also encourages appropriate expression, or **prosody**. When the teacher, the student, or an entire student body reads aloud, students become more exposed to the use of prosody; therefore, their reading expression is strengthened. When teachers read aloud, they model prosody, which cues students to the social norms of pace, pauses, inflection, emotion, and tone when reading different types of text. In **choral reading**, all students in the class read a passage aloud together, which allows them to hear text being read accurately and with good pacing and phrasing. By having students listen to recordings of themselves reading, teachers promote independent judgment and goal setting.

Reading theaters also support prosody. During reading theater instruction, students are assigned a character in a play. The emphasis is reading aloud with a purpose. Students use prosody to share their interpretations and understandings of their assigned characters' personalities and roles.

Phrase-cued reading is a third strategy that aids the development of prosody. During phrase-cued reading, teachers read a text aloud and mark where they pause or show intonation, emphasis, tone, inflections, and/or expression.

How to Address a Range of Needs

Several strategies can be implemented to assist English Language Learners, speakers of nonstandard English, advanced learners, and readers who have reading difficulties or disabilities. However, it's always important to provide each student with reading materials and strategies that are appropriate for their specific reading level and area of concern.

Struggling readers, students with reading difficulties or disabilities, and students with special needs benefit from direct instruction and feedback that teaches decoding and analysis of unknown words, automaticity in key sight words, and correct expression and phrasing. These learners also benefit from oral support. This may be provided through scaffolded reading, choral reading, partner reading, books on tape, and computer programs. Teachers should consistently offer opportunities for students to practice repeated reading and should gradually introduce more challenging reading levels as students progress.

English Language Learners and speakers of nonstandard English benefit from explicit instruction in vocabulary development in order to aid accuracy, rate, and reading comprehension. Providing ample opportunities to read orally with a scaffolding approach, which gradually increases the difficulty of the work and slowly asks for more independence from the student, also helps this group. For instance, teachers may read a short passage and have students immediately read it back to them. Direct instruction in English intonation patterns, syntax, and punctuation are effective tools in assisting English language learners with the development of prosody.

In order to broaden and enhance fluency for advanced learners, teachers should gradually introduce more advanced texts across several content areas.

Continued Assessment of Student Fluency

Assessment of fluency must include entry-level assessments, progress monitoring, and summative assessments of accuracy, rate, and prosody. The results should be analyzed and interpreted in order to adjust instruction and provide struggling readers with proper interventions. Regular assessments also help teachers to construct differentiated instruction in order to address the fluency needs of advanced learners.

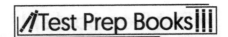

Assessing Students' Word-Reading Accuracy

Running records, widely used fluency assessments, allow teachers to document error patterns in reading accuracy as students read benchmark books. As the student reads aloud, the teacher holds a copy of the same text and records any omissions, mispronunciations, and substitutions. With this information, teachers can determine which fluency strategies a student does or doesn't employ.

Using Timed Contextual Oral Reading to Assess Fluency and Rate

Assessment of reading rate often begins with sight-word reading automaticity. Automaticity assessment may also include the decoding of non-words in order to determine if a student is able to decode words using sound-syllable correspondence.

Among the most commonly used measurements of reading rate is oral contextual timed reading. During a **timed reading**, the number of errors made within a given amount of time is recorded. This data can be used to identify if a student's rate is improving and if reading rate falls within the recommended fluency rates for the student's grade level. If a student's reading rate is below average, any of the previously identified research-based, systematic, explicit strategies that improve fluency with respect to rate may be applied.

One common timed assessment for reading accuracy is the **WCPM**, the words-correct-per-minute assessment. The teacher presents an unfamiliar text to a student and asks the student to read aloud for one minute. As the student reads, the teacher records any omissions, mispronunciations, or substitutions. These errors are subtracted by the total number of words in the text to determine a score, which is then compared to oral reading fluency norms. With this assessment, teachers can select the appropriate level of text for each student.

Recommended Reading Fluency Rates		
Grade	**Semester**	**Correct Words Per Minute**
First Grade	Winter	38
	Spring	40–60
Second Grade	Fall	55
	Winter	73–79
	Spring	81–93
Third Grade	Fall	79
	Winter	83–92
	Spring	100–115
Fourth Grade	Fall	91–99
	Winter	98–113
	Spring	106–119
Fifth Grade	Fall	105
	Winter	109–118
	Spring	118–128

Assessing Prosody Through Observation of Connected-Text Reading

In order to assess prosody, a teacher listens for inflection, expression, and pauses as the student reads a connected text aloud. The Integrate Reading Performance Record Oral Reading Fluency Scale designed by the National Assessment of Educational Progress (NAEP) is also used to assess prosody. Students at

levels 3 and 4 are considered fluent in prosody, while students at levels 1 and 2 are considered to be non-fluent.

Level 4: Reads mainly in large phrase groups. The structure of the story is intact and the author's syntax is consistent, even if there are some deviations from the text. Most of the story is read with expression.

Level 3: Reads mainly in three- or four-word phrase groups. Majority of phrasing is appropriate and preserves syntax of the author. Little expression is present with interpreting the text.

Level 2: Reads two-word phrases with some three- or four-word groupings. Word-by-word reading may occur. Some word groupings may seem awkward, indicating that the student is not paying attention to the larger context.

Level 1: Reads word-by-word. Some occasional two-or-three word phrases may be present, but they are not frequent or they don't preserve meaningful syntax.

Oral Vocabulary and the Process of Decoding Written Words

Vocabulary, both oral and written, depends largely on phonology or the ability to understand how sounds work in language. Obviously, this understanding first occurs through oral communication and a student's understanding of words and their meaning when spoken. More specifically, a student's ability to decode oral language creates phonemic awareness, or the ability to work with individual sounds within words, which translates to the student's ability to decode written language. Similarly, semantics (words) and syntax (usage) in oral communication help establish the foundations for reading.

Familiarizing students with the sounds made by letters or letter combinations in the spoken language as well as learning syllables, rhyme, and rime (the string of letters that follow the onset of a word) is key to developing their decoding skills. The first step to doing this is to teach students individual letter sounds. You may choose to work through the alphabet, but also starting with a child's name is a great technique as the child will be more invested. Try to avoid teaching similar-sounding letters at the same time, as this can be confusing. The letters *B* and *P*, for example, have similar sounds and our mouths make similar shapes to pronounce them, so wait until students have gained familiarity with one letter before moving to the next.

A great game to play with students is to put picture and letter cards out on a table. Then have students say out loud what the picture is, listen for the letter sound, and group items that start with the same letter together. This exercise also allows you to teach onset (the first letter or sound of a word). From there, the lessons can move into rhyming, which helps teach students rime, or how the letters follow the onset. This can also be taught with games as simple as identifying an emotion, such as *fear*, and having students identify words that rhyme. Students may come up with *near, gear,* or *tear.* Games like this can be played with just about any item in a classroom, such as a pen or a wall. These lessons help students learn to identify the ways letters work together in different parts of a word, so that when they try to sound words out later, the task is more manageable.

Research suggests that the ability to translate all these building blocks of spoken language results in stronger readers. Further, children with robust oral vocabularies and the ability to form varied sentences demonstrate stronger reading skills, which further establishes the connection between oral language and reading. To foster this relationship and connection, early instruction should include activities that include rhyming games, syllable identification, onset and rime identification, and blending phonemes.

Terminology Associated with Phonics

In understanding and working with phonics, there are specific terms and concepts it is vital to understand. Phonics itself teaches language and reading skills by focusing on letters and their specific sounds as well as the sounds made by common letter combinations. With the ability to recognize the patterns and combinations, early readers can begin to decode unfamiliar words.

Specific vocabulary includes:

Digraph: Two letters that, when combined, make a singular sound. Examples of digraphs include: *sh*, *th*, *ch*, and *ph*.

Grapheme: A grapheme is a symbol that is written that represents a sound (phoneme). In other words, it can be one or more written letters that represent a singular sound. For example, both the letter *s* and the letter combination *igh* (as in *sigh*) are graphemes.

Morpheme: This refers to the smallest unit of meaning in a word. Morphemes are further broken down into root words and affixes. For example, *at* is a root word, and it can't be broken down further without changing the meaning. Affixes include suffixes and prefixes; they can ascribe meaning as well. For example, both *un* and *s* add meaning to a word and are considered morphemes.

Onset: This refers to the first consonants or consonant blends in a word. For example, in the word *game*, the letter *g* is the onset; in the word *brake*, the letters *br* are the onset.

Phoneme: This refers to the smallest distinct unit of sound in a language. For example, the *b* in the word *bat* is a phoneme. It has a distinct sound all on its own.

Rime: These are the letters and sounds that follow the onset and can be a mix of vowels and consonants. For example, as noted above, in the word *game*, *g* is the onset, and so *ame* is the rime. In the word *brake*, *br* is the onset and *ake* is the rime.

Schwa: The schwa is a vowel sound sometimes created in the unstressed syllable of a word and typically makes a "uh" sound. For example, in the word *bacon*, the *o* is a schwa.

Vowel digraph: A vowel digraph is two letter vowels that create one sound. For example, the *ie* in a word like *thief*.

Phonics Skills and Fluency in Individual Students

The primary goal of phonics education in early readers is to develop familiarity with the relationships between sounds and letters or letter combinations. Through this familiarity, students become stronger readers as they gain confidence in decoding new words and sounding out new combinations. That developed reading strength and confidence are the foundation for fluency.

There are multiple methods to achieving fluency, but the basis of any method should include significant vocabulary acquisition and development through oral communication and reading aloud. These should be paired with group discussions that allow students to further explore what they have heard in terms of meaning, context, and language.

Ideally, reading lessons are paired with specific phonics instruction that includes recognition of alphabetic principles so that students learn to quickly identify individual letters and the sounds they

make, followed by letter pairs and blends and the sounds those make. While reading aloud with students, teachers should be sure to have students identify letters and sounds in words, particularly those that are new. Phonics instruction should start with monosyllabic words and then move into multisyllabic words, working with phonemes and morphemes to be sure students understand the basic structure of words themselves, enabling them to decode the new and unfamiliar.

To have reading instruction continue to build phonic skills, have students work with rhyming words. Teachers should establish the different units of sound (onset vs. rime), split words into syllables, and identify phonemes in spoken and written words. As with other instruction, patterns should include teacher-led reading, group reading, and finally independent reading.

The written portion, at this point, should include activities centered on print awareness (environmental print is valuable here), letter and letter combination sound recognition (flashcards may be useful), and other activities that engage students in early reading, writing, and spelling. Further, students should begin participating in read-aloud activities, similar to those that establish and build automaticity, and begin learning words by sight.

Word Analysis Skills and Strategies

Word Analysis and Word Recognition Automaticity

Phonics and decoding skills aid the analysis of new words. Word analysis is the ability to recognize the relationships between the spelling, syllabication, and pronunciation of new and/or unfamiliar words. Having a clear understanding of word structure, orthography, and the meaning of morphemes also aids in the analysis of new words.

However, not all words follow predictable patterns of phonics, morphology, or orthography. Such irregular words must be committed to memory and are called sight words.

Phonics skills, syllabic skills, structural analysis, word analysis, and memorization of sight words lead to word recognition automaticity. Word recognition is the ability to correctly and automatically recognize words in or out of context. Word recognition is a prerequisite for fluent reading and reading comprehension.

Word Analysis Skills, Fluency, and Reading Comprehension

These three concepts—word analysis skills, fluency, and reading comprehension—are interconnected and inter-reliant. Word analysis refers to a student's ability to identify and define words; comprehension refers to the student's ability to then understand those words. Without analysis and comprehension, students can't read fluently. Conversely, if a student can recognize words and read fluently, this also suggests a higher level of comprehension. However, if a student can successfully decode with fluency but reads aloud without expression, there may be issues of comprehension. Rather than being a linear connection, the three concepts are more interrelated like a triangle.

Word analysis skills, which should be considered as contributing to comprehension, include identification of morphemes, recognition of common affixes, knowledge of root words and their etymology, sight recognition, and recognition of homographs. All these skills lend themselves to a student's ability to see a word and effortlessly recognize how it is pronounced or read. Even if a student can successfully use these strategies, if a text is well above their standard reading level, their **fluency**

level may decrease. The same is true if the text is simple, in that fluency (and comprehension) will naturally increase. Increases in word analysis skills contribute to automaticity and fluency.

Comprehension skills, which then contribute to fluency, include background knowledge, vocabulary, sentence structure, syntax, reasoning, and knowledge of genre and style. A student's ability to bring this knowledge to reading demonstrates an increasingly strategic reader. That said, research suggests that comprehension and fluency share a bidirectional relationship in that each can contribute to the other; so, as a student gains word analysis skills and comprehension, fluency should naturally follow, and, as suggested, fluency can then increase comprehension.

Common Morphemes

Morphemes are defined as the smallest unit of a word that has meaning. The morpheme must not be able to be broken into smaller units with the same meaning, and it maintains that meaning despite its context.

Morphemes can be further categorized as base or root morphemes and affixes. **Base or root morphemes** give the word their primary meaning and are also called **free morphemes** because they can stand alone and have a specific meaning. For example, *cat* is a base morpheme. It cannot be broken down and it provides the primary meaning. However, if we add the letter *s*, *cats*, *s* is a morpheme in that it is now the smallest unit of the word that provides a plural meaning.

The other category of morphemes is **bound morphemes**, which are affixes. Bound morphemes must be connected to another word and do not hold meaning on their own. In the above example, *s* has meaning but cannot stand alone. It must be bound to the free morpheme, *cat*.

The most **common prefixes** in English are:

- re-: recount, recover, redress

- dis-: disown, discover, dismount

- over-: overjoyed, overcome, overworked

- un-: uncover, unjust, uncomfortable

- mis-: mistake, misrepresent, mishap

- out-: outtake, outcropping, outspoken

The most **common suffixes** in English are:

- -tion: action, publication, attention

- -ity: disparity, clarity, compatibility

- -er: leaner, cleaner, meaner

- -ness: kindness, darkness, fierceness

- -ism: Marxism, capitalism, socialism

- -ment: shipment, fragment, argument

- -ant: descendant, distant, miscreant

- -ship: relationship, friendship, leadership

- -age: patronage, baggage, package

- -ery: nursery, battery, misery

Teaching morphemes is essential in having students learn how to break down words for reading and comprehension. Because the meaning of many affixes does not change, regardless of the root word they are attached to, once students recognize them and their meaning, they are better able to break the word down for pronunciation, identify the root, and decode meaning, which all contributes to their reading fluency and overall comprehension skills.

Having students learn to break words down into morphemes will help them realize that unfamiliar words contain parts that are familiar. Exercises should include this type of activity.

Another breakdown activity involves giving students complex words that contain multiple morphemes (a root or base and affixes). After breaking down the complex words, have the students research the etymology.

Students can also work with word lists and sort words by base or root words and affixes. Similarly, they can work with morpheme cards and put words together using affixes to create new words as a word building exercise, almost like the game *Boggle*.

Common Prefixes and Suffixes and their Meanings

By analyzing and understanding Latin, Greek, and Anglo-Saxon word roots, prefixes, and suffixes one can better understand word meanings. Of course, people can always look words up in a dictionary or thesaurus if available, but meaning can often be gleaned on the spot if the writer learns to dissect and examine words.

A word can consist of the following:

> root
> root + suffix
> prefix + root
> prefix + root + suffix

For example, if someone was unfamiliar with the word *submarine* they could break the word into its parts.

> prefix + root
> sub + marine

It can be determined that *sub* means *below* as in *subway* and *subpar*. Additionally, one can determine that *marine* refers to *the sea* as in *marine life*. Thus, it can be figured that *submarine* refers to something below the water.

43

Roots

Roots are the basic components of words. Many roots can stand alone as individual words, but others must be combined with a prefix or suffix to be a word. For example, *calc* is a root but it needs a suffix to be an actual word (*calcium*).

Prefixes

A **prefix** is a word, letter, or number that is placed before another. It adjusts or qualifies the root word's meaning. When written alone, prefixes are followed by a dash to indicate that the root word follows. Some of the most common prefixes are the following:

Prefix	Meaning	Example
dis-	not or opposite of	disabled
in-, im-, il-, ir-	not	illiterate
re-	again	return
un-	not	unpredictable
anti-	against	antibacterial
fore-	before	forefront
mis-	wrongly	misunderstand
non-	not	nonsense
over-	more than normal	overabundance
pre-	before	preheat
super-	above	superman

Suffixes

A **suffix** is a letter or group of letters added at the end of a word to form another word. The word created from the root and suffix is either a different tense of the same root (*help* + *ed* = *helped*) or a new word (*help* + *ful* = *helpful*). When written alone, suffixes are preceded by a dash to indicate that the root word comes before.

Some of the most common prefixes are the following:

Suffix	Meaning	Example
-ed	makes a verb past tense	washed
-ing	makes a verb a present participle verb	washing
-ly	to make characteristic of	lovely
-s/es	to make more than one	chairs, boxes
-able	can be done	deplorable
-al	having characteristics of	comical
-est	comparative	greatest
-ful	full of	wonderful
-ism	belief in	communism
-less	without	faithless
-ment	action or process	accomplishment

44

Suffix	Meaning	Example
-ness	state of	happi*ness*
-ize, -ise	to render, to make	steril*ize*, advert*ise*
-cede/ceed/sede	go	concede, proceed, supersede

Here are some helpful tips:

When adding a suffix that starts with a vowel (for example, *-ed*) to a one-syllable root whose vowel has a short sound and ends in a consonant (for example, *stun*), double the final consonant of the root (*n*).

stun + ed = stun*n*ed

Exception: If the past tense verb ends in *x* such as *box*, do not double the *x*.

box + ed = boxed

If adding a suffix that starts with a vowel (*-er*) to a multi-syllable word ending in a consonant (*begin*), double the consonant (*n*).

begin + er = begin*n*er

If a short vowel is followed by two or more consonants in a word such as *i+t+c+h = itch,* do <u>not</u> double the last consonant.

itch + ed = itched

If adding a suffix that starts with a vowel (*-ing*) to a word ending in *e* (for example, *name*), that word's final *e* is generally (but not always) dropped.

name + ing = naming

exception: manage + able = manageable

If adding a suffix that starts with a consonant (*-ness*) to a word ending in *e* (*complete*), the *e* generally (but not always) remains.

complete + ness = completeness

exception: judge + ment = judgment

There is great diversity on handling words that end in *y*. For words ending in a vowel + y, nothing changes in the original word.

play + ed = played

For words ending in a consonant + *y*, change the *y* to *i* when adding any suffix except for *–ing*.

marry + ed = married

marry + ing = marrying

45

Knowledge of Latin and Greek Roots that Form English Words

Understanding the meaning of a part of a word can aid in understanding the meaning of the entire word. Knowledge of Greek, Latin, and Anglo-Saxon roots and affixes can help students to decode the meaning of unfamiliar words and build vocabulary. Some examples follow:

Greek Root	Meaning	Latin Root	Meaning	Anglo-Saxon Root	Meaning
cosm	universe	bene	good	ber	carry
dec	ten	clar	clear	kno	skill
macro	large	ject	throw	tru	faithful
poli	city	mot	move	ward	guard

Syllabication as a Word Identification Strategy

Reading competence of multisyllabic words is accomplished through phonics skills that are accompanied with a reader's ability to recognize morphological structures within words. Structural analysis is a word recognition skill that focuses on the meaning of word parts, or morphemes, during the introduction of a new word. Therefore, the instruction of structural analysis focuses on the recognition and application of morphemes. Students can use structural analysis skills to find familiar word parts within an unfamiliar word in order to decode the word and determine the definition of the new word. Identification and association of such word segments also aids the proper pronunciation and spelling of new multisyllabic words.

The following table identifies the six basic syllable patterns that should be explicitly taught during syllabic instruction:

Basic Syllable Patterns		
Name of Syllable Type	Characteristics of Syllable Type	Examples
Closed	A syllable with a single vowel closed in by a consonant.	*lab, bog, an*
Open	A syllable that ends with a single vowel. Note that the letter *y* acts as a vowel.	*go, me, sly*
Vowel-Consonant-Silent *e*	A syllable with a single vowel followed by a consonant then *e*.	*like, rake, note, obese*
Vowel Teams	A syllable that has two consecutive vowels. Note that the letters *w* and *y* act as vowels.	*meat, pertain, bay, toad, window*
R-controlled	A syllable with one or two vowels followed by the letter *r*.	*car, jar, fir, sir, collar, turmoil*
Consonant le (-al, -el). Also called final stable	A syllable that has a consonant followed by the letters *le, al,* or *el*.	*puddle, stable, uncle, bridal, pedal*

46

Basic Syllable Patterns		
Name of Syllable Type	**Characteristics of Syllable Type**	**Examples**
Other final stable syllables	A syllable at the end of words can be taught as a recognizable unit such as *cious, age, ture, tion,* or *sion.*	*pension, elation, puncture, stumpage, fictitious*

Syllables and Morphemes in Relation to Spelling Patterns

Spelling and reading rely on some of the same strategies for word analysis. Therefore, they can be used to support one another in the classroom.

A significant majority of English words follows a predictable pattern that students should be able to recognize when they have worked with phonemes. More specifically, words with regular spelling patterns can be sounded out by identifying the individual sounds in the words. Each sound, therefore, corresponds to the letter that makes that sound. The **sound-it-out strategy** is the primary method of teaching the spelling words that follow the regular spelling pattern. For longer words, this task is significantly more difficult. Therefore, breaking the word down into its morphemes or by syllable is a better strategy. After breaking the word down, students can identify individual sounds and sound it out.

Applying phonics lessons to spelling, and moving from easiest to more difficult, students should be taught spelling words in a specific order that builds on their skills.

Start with words that are formed with consonants and short vowel sounds like *put, cat,* and *mat.* Then move into consonant blends and digraphs like *blue, shoe,* and *clock.* Next, move into words with long vowels (they make the sound of the letter) and a final *e* such as *cane, gave,* and *cake.* Once students have grasped these spellings, especially the final *e,* move into long vowels with digraphs such as *blame, grain,* and *breeze.* Each of these steps is progressive, building on the skill the students learned before. Once they have success here, students are ready for spelling words with other vowel patterns such as *these, shield,* and *radio.* These words do not follow a set pattern and they combine vowel sounds, so they are a bit trickier for students to "sound out."

Next is introducing the patterns associated with different types of syllables. Syllables follow six patterns:

Closed syllables: A closed syllable is a short vowel followed by a consonant like *on* or *rat.*

Open syllables: An open syllable ends with a long vowel like *cry* or *go.*

Vowel-consonant-e syllables: These syllables end in a silent e preceded by a consonant and a long vowel like *cute* or *home.*

Diphthongs (vowel teams): These words include two vowels next to one another that are pronounced as one letter like *eight* or *through.*

R-controlled syllables: These words have at least one vowel followed by the letter *r* like *her* or *fur.*

Consonant-le syllables: These syllables have no vowel sound. They are consonant blends followed by a silent *e* like *table* or *maple.*

47

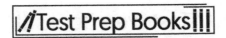

Affixes are the final spelling pattern to review with students going over common suffixes like *-tion* and *-ous* and prefixes like *pre-* and *con-*.

The goal here is to teach students to identify similar patterns in words. Thus, when they sound out new words, patterns and pronunciations are familiar.

Techniques for Identifying Compound Words

Compound words are words that take two smaller words, put them together, and create a new word. A student's understanding of morphemes is key here, as their ability to identify the smallest unit of meaning in a word will help them isolate the two smaller words that are combined.

There are multiple strategies for teaching compound words. For early learners, it may be easiest to begin with pictures that show the combination of the words. Creating flashcards with a picture on one side and the word on the other allows room for growth with this exercise. More specifically, it allows instruction to move from pictures to a combination of pictures and words and finish with only the words. For example, teachers can show a picture of a cat and a picture of a fish and lead the students to create the compound word *catfish*. This is a good way to introduce the concept.

Once students have mastered creating compound words, identifying them in texts will be easier. In texts, students can be asked to find longer words and determine whether they are compound words. If they are, the student should be able to break the word into two smaller words. They can then create a chart that identifies the first small word, the second small word, and what the two words mean individually as well as in combination. This helps students learn how to read the compound words.

Very young readers should learn about **closed compound words** first. These are identified by the two smaller words put together with no space in between, like *treehouse*. Once they master these, instruction can introduce **open compound words**. This concept is a bit more difficult for early readers as the words are separated by a space, though the meaning changes when the two words are placed together. A great example of an open compound word is *ice cream*. Students will need to learn to identify these based on what looks correct and memorization. However, classroom instruction can put these two compound word styles in practice sentences and have students identify open and closed compound words.

The final type of compound word is the **hyphenated compound**. These are smaller words joined by a hyphen such as *jack-o-lantern* or *long-term*. However, learning how to use hyphenated compound words is a lesson that should be accompanied by grammar lessons in which students learn to identify parts of speech to better determine when a hyphen should be used, such as compound adjectives that are followed by the noun they modify. As such, these more complex compound words should only be introduced once there is mastery of the other types of compound words.

Homographs

Homographs are words that are spelled the same but have different meanings, such as *rose* (which can mean the flower or the past tense of *rise*) and *fly* (which can mean the insect or the act of taking flight). To begin teaching students about this often confusing element of the English language, teachers can ask if students have encountered homographs before and see if students can brainstorm a list. Once students have exhausted their recollection, explain the word *homograph* and its connection to the exercise they've just completed.

48

Next, from the list students have created, have students draw a picture of each of the meanings. From there, provide students with a list of homographs and have them move from drawing the pictures to writing the words out.

From there, instruction can move into more complex exercises than word recognition, such as using context to decode which meaning the word has in a sentence. One strategy for this is to teach students riddles that involve homographs. Riddles can include word decoding, such as *"How do you make a slow horse fast? Don't let him eat."* In this riddle, the play is on the word *fast*, and teachers can discuss with students the double meaning and how it makes this riddle funny. Teachers can also ask students to come up with the homographs on their own. For example, teachers can ask students to figure out the homograph from this clue: *"Outside on a diamond, a sphere you will throw; dress up and go dance, Cinderella did go."* Students can work in pairs or teams to come up with the word *ball*. The goal here is for students to start to examine how the context in a sentence helps them determine which meaning of the word is appropriate.

Context Clues

Familiarity with common prefixes, suffixes, and root words assists tremendously in unraveling the meaning of an unfamiliar word and making an educated guess as to its meaning. However, some words do not contain many easily-identifiable clues that point to their meaning. In this case, rather than looking at the elements within the word, it is useful to consider elements around the word—i.e., its context. **Context** refers to the other words and information within the sentence or surrounding sentences that indicate the unknown word's probable meaning. The following sentences provide context for the potentially-unfamiliar word *quixotic*:

> Rebecca had never been one to settle into a predictable, ordinary life. Her quixotic personality led her to leave behind a job with a prestigious law firm in Manhattan and move halfway around the world to pursue her dream of becoming a sushi chef in Tokyo.

A reader unfamiliar with the word *quixotic* doesn't have many clues to use in terms of affixes or root meaning. The suffix *–ic* indicates that the word is an adjective, but that is it. In this case, then, a reader would need to look at surrounding information to obtain some clues about the word. Other adjectives in the passage include *predictable* and *ordinary*, things that Rebecca was definitely not, as indicated by "Rebecca had never been one to settle." Thus, a first clue might be that *quixotic* means the opposite of predictable.

The second sentence doesn't offer any other modifier of *personality* other than *quixotic*, but it does include a story that reveals further information about her personality. She had a stable, respectable job, but she decided to give it up to follow her dream. Combining these two ideas together, then—unpredictable and dream-seeking—gives the reader a general idea of what *quixotic* probably means. In fact, the root of the word is the character Don Quixote, a romantic dreamer who goes on an impulsive adventure.

While context clues are useful for making an approximate definition for newly-encountered words, these types of clues also come in handy when encountering common words that have multiple meanings. The word *reservation* is used differently in each the following sentences:

> A: That restaurant is booked solid for the next month; it's impossible to make a reservation unless you know somebody.

49

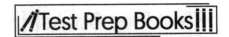

B: The hospital plans to open a branch office inside the reservation to better serve Native American patients who cannot easily travel to the main hospital fifty miles away.

C: Janet Clark is a dependable, knowledgeable worker, and I recommend her for the position of team leader without reservation.

All three sentences use the word to express different meanings. In fact, most words in English have more than one meaning—sometimes meanings that are completely different from one another. Thus, context can provide clues as to which meaning is appropriate in a given situation. A quick search in the dictionary reveals several possible meanings for *reservation*:

1. An exception or qualification

2. A tract of public land set aside, such as for the use of American Indian tribes

3. An arrangement for accommodations, such as in a hotel, on a plane, or at a restaurant

Sentence A mentions a restaurant, making the third definition the correct one in this case. In sentence B, some context clues include Native Americans, as well as the implication that a reservation is a place— "inside the reservation," both of which indicate that the second definition should be used here. Finally, sentence C uses *without reservation* to mean "completely" or "without exception," so the first definition can be applied here.

Using context clues in this way can be especially useful for words that have multiple, widely varying meanings. If a word has more than one definition and two of those definitions are the opposite of each other, it is known as an **auto-antonym**—a word that can also be its own antonym. In the case of auto-antonyms, context clues are crucial to determine which definition to employ in a given sentence. For example, the word *sanction* can either mean "to approve or allow" or "a penalty." Approving and penalizing have opposite meanings, so *sanction* is an example of an auto-antonym. The following sentences reflect the distinction in meaning:

A: In response to North Korea's latest nuclear weapons test, world leaders have called for harsher sanctions to punish the country for its actions.

B: The general has sanctioned a withdrawal of troops from the area.

A context clue can be found in sentence A, which mentions "to punish." A punishment is similar to a penalty, so sentence A is using the word *sanction* according to this definition.

Other examples of auto-antonyms include *oversight*—"to supervise something" or "a missed detail," *resign*—"to quit" or "to sign again, as a contract," and *screen*—"to show" or "to conceal." For these types of words, recognizing context clues is an important way to avoid misinterpreting the sentence's meaning.

Syntax
Syntax refers to the arrangement of words, phrases, and clauses to form a sentence. Knowledge of syntax can also give insight into a word's meaning. The section above considered several examples using the word *reservation* and applied context clues to determine the word's appropriate meaning in each sentence. Here is an example of how the placement of a word can impact its meaning and grammatical function:

A: The development team has reserved the conference room for today.

B: Her quiet and reserved nature is sometimes misinterpreted as unfriendliness when people first meet her.

In addition to using *reserved* to mean different things, each sentence also uses the word to serve a different grammatical function. In sentence A, *reserved* is part of the verb phrase *has reserved*, indicating the meaning "to set aside for a particular use." In sentence B, *reserved* acts as a modifier within the noun phrase "her quiet and reserved nature." Because the word is being used as an adjective to describe a personality characteristic, it calls up a different definition of the word—"restrained or lacking familiarity with others." As this example shows, the function of a word within the overall sentence structure can allude to its meaning. It is also useful to refer to the earlier chart about suffixes and parts of speech as another clue into what grammatical function a word is serving in a sentence.

Analyzing Nuances of Word Meaning and Figures of Speech

By now, it should be apparent that language is not as simple as one word directly correlated to one meaning. Rather, one word can express a vast array of diverse meanings, and similar meanings can be expressed through different words. However, there are very few words that express exactly the same meaning. For this reason, it is important to be able to pick up on the nuances of word meaning.

Many words contain two levels of meaning: connotation and denotation as discussed previously in the informational texts and rhetoric section. A word's **denotation** is its most literal meaning—the definition that can readily be found in the dictionary. A word's **connotation** includes all of its emotional and cultural associations.

In literary writing, authors rely heavily on connotative meaning to create mood and characterization. The following are two descriptions of a rainstorm:

A: The rain slammed against the windowpane and the wind howled through the fireplace. A pair of hulking oaks next to the house cast eerie shadows as their branches trembled in the wind.

B: The rain pattered against the windowpane and the wind whistled through the fireplace. A pair of stately oaks next to the house cast curious shadows as their branches swayed in the wind.

Description A paints a creepy picture for readers with strongly emotional words like *slammed*, connoting force and violence. *Howled* connotes pain or wildness, and *eerie* and *trembled* connote fear. Overall, the connotative language in this description serves to inspire fear and anxiety.

However, as can be seen in description B, swapping out a few key words for those with different connotations completely changes the feeling of the passage. *Slammed* is replaced with the more cheerful *pattered*, and *hulking* has been swapped out for *stately*. Both words imply something large, but *hulking* is more intimidating whereas *stately* is more respectable. *Curious* and *swayed* seem more playful than the language used in the earlier description. Although both descriptions represent roughly the same situation, the nuances of the emotional language used throughout the passages create a very different sense for readers.

Selective choice of connotative language can also be extremely impactful in other forms of writing, such as editorials or persuasive texts. Through connotative language, writers reveal their biases and opinions while trying to inspire feelings and actions in readers:

Parents won't stop complaining about standardized tests.

Parents continue to raise concerns about standardized tests.

Readers should be able to identify the nuance in meaning between these two sentences. The first one carries a more negative feeling, implying that parents are being bothersome or whiny. Readers of the second sentence, though, might come away with the feeling that parents are concerned and involved in their children's education. Again, the aggregate of even subtle cues can combine to give a specific emotional impression to readers, so from an early age, students should be aware of how language can be used to influence readers' opinions.

Another form of non-literal expression can be found in **figures of speech**. As with connotative language, figures of speech tend to be shared within a cultural group and may be difficult to pick up on for learners outside of that group. In some cases, a figure of speech may be based on the literal denotation of the words it contains, but in other cases, a figure of speech is far removed from its literal meaning. A case in point is **irony**, where what is said is the exact opposite of what is meant:

> The new tax plan is poorly planned, based on faulty economic data, and unable to address the financial struggles of middle-class families. Yet legislators remain committed to passing this brilliant proposal.

When the writer refers to the proposal as brilliant, the opposite is implied—the plan is "faulty" and "poorly planned." By using irony, the writer means that the proposal is anything but brilliant by using the word in a non-literal sense.

Another figure of speech is **hyperbole**—extreme exaggeration or overstatement. Statements like "I love you to the moon and back" or "Let's be friends for a million years" utilize hyperbole to convey a greater depth of emotion, without literally committing oneself to space travel or a life of immortality.

Figures of speech may sometimes use one word in place of another. **Synecdoche**, for example, uses a part of something to refer to its whole. The expression "Don't hurt a hair on her head!" implies protecting more than just an individual hair, but rather her entire body. "The art teacher is training a class of Picassos" uses Picasso, one individual notable artist, to stand in for the entire category of talented artists. Another figure of speech using word replacement is **metonymy**, where a word is replaced with something closely associated to it. For example, news reports may use the word *Washington* to refer to the American government or *the crown* to refer to the British monarch.

Word Analysis Skills and Fluency in Individual Students

The teaching of structural and syllabic analysis begins with direct instruction of morphemes and the six basic syllable patterns. During the initial stage of instruction, the definition and differences of the two terms need to be addressed. The origins of words are also discussed. Students are asked to memorize the meaning of morphemes (e.g., *dis-* = lack of). Memorization of morphemes and their meanings will aid in identification of new vocabulary terms and the spelling of multisyllabic words.

The second stage of structural and syllabic analysis instruction involves the teaching of multisyllabic words that are formed by adding a common prefix or suffix to a base word. Online and offline resources, such as dictionaries and thesauruses, can be used as tools to provide information about the morphemes and syllables within words. Prefixes, suffixes, and bases can be written on sticky notes. The sticky notes can be rearranged in order to form multisyllabic words.

52

Next, students are asked to identify the morphemes and syllables in words. This can be done via whole-to-part instruction. Students underline words within sentences that share the same prefix, suffix, or root. Then, the students read the underlined words to identify commonalities. Prefixes are usually the first to be spotted by young readers, followed by suffixes. Contextual clues and scaffolding provided by the teacher are used to derive a definition of the underlined or highlighted morpheme(s). Similarly, students can be asked to break all the syllables apart so that the entire words' definitions can be inferred.

Finally, students are taught how to use their obtained knowledge of structural analysis and syllable patterns to spell multisyllabic words.

Syllabic and structural analysis and orthographic knowledge must support the decoding and spelling of multisyllabic words and words that follow more complex orthographic patterns or rules among a full range of learners in the classroom. In this section, differentiated strategies are identified that promote these skills in students who struggle with reading, disabled and special-needs students, English-language learners (ELLs), speakers of nonstandard English, and advanced learners.

Instruction in these areas for students who struggle with reading, disabled students, or students with special needs should be streamlined, systematic, and explicit. Focus should be committed toward essential skills and knowledge. For example, emphasis should be placed on syllable patterns, affixes, and related orthographic patterns that occur with the highest frequencies. Such instruction should occur frequently and at predictable times. Concepts and skills that are lacking in these students should be targeted through remediation and routine practice that employs a variety of concrete examples. Visual, auditory, kinesthetic, and tactile techniques should be used when providing additional oral practice with new words. Oral practice can occur through purposeful listening, language interactions, and shared reading or writing experiences.

Instruction of these areas can also be differentiated for ELLs and speakers of nonstandard English. For these students, teachers should capitalize on the transfer of related syllabic and structural analysis and/or orthographic knowledge from a student's primary language into the English language. In this way, extra attention and instructional emphasis can be applied toward the direct instruction of nontransferable roots and affixes.

Advanced learners benefit from phonics skills, sight word knowledge, and spelling of single-syllable words with increased complexity. The breadth of current knowledge and skills should be extended and instruction should occur at a faster pace.

Practice Quiz

1. What is the best definition of connotation?
   a. The literal meaning of a word
   b. A figure of speech
   c. An idiom
   d. The meaning of a word including its emotional and cultural associations

2. Phonemic awareness, phonics, fluency, vocabulary, and comprehension are the five basic elements of what?
   a. Phonics
   b. Spelling instruction
   c. Reading education
   d. Genre

3. A child reads the story "*Little Red Riding Hood*" aloud. He easily pronounces the words, uses an apprehensive tone to show that the main character should not be leaving the path, adds a scary voice for the Big Bad Wolf, and reads the story at a pace that engages the class. What are these promising signs of?
   a. Reading fluency
   b. Phonemic awareness
   c. Reading comprehension
   d. Working memory

4. A student is trying to read the word *preferred*. She first recognizes the word *red* at the end, then sounds out the rest of the word by breaking it down into "pre," then "fer," then "red." Finally she puts it together and says "preferred." This student is displaying what attribute?
   a. Phonemic awareness
   b. Phonics
   c. Fluency
   d. Vocabulary

5. A class silently reads a passage on the American Revolution. Once they are done, the teacher asks the students to name the two sides who were fighting, the reason they were fighting, and the winner. What skill is the teacher gauging?
   a. Orthographic development
   b. Fluency
   c. Comprehension
   d. Phonics

See answers on the next page.

Answer Explanations

1. D: The connotation of a word is the meaning of a word including all of its emotional and cultural associations. One example is the difference between words such as hulking and stately. Choice *A* is the definition of denotation rather than connotation. Choices *B* and *C* are incorrect because connotation does not define the meaning of a figure of speech or of an idiom. Rather, understanding these devices must be practiced and learned (for figures of speech) or memorized (for idioms).

2. C: The five basic components of reading education are phonemic awareness, phonics, fluency, vocabulary, and comprehension.

3. A: If a child can accurately read text with consistent speed and appropriate expression while demonstrating comprehension, the child is said to have reading fluency skills. Without the ability to read fluently, a child's reading comprehension, Choice *C*, will be limited.

4. B: Phonics is the ability to apply letter-sound relationships and letter patterns in order to accurately pronounce written words. Phonemic awareness is the understanding that words are comprised of a combination of sounds. Fluency is an automatic recognition and accurate interpretation of text. Vocabulary is the body of words that a person knows.

5. C: Comprehension is the level of content understanding that a student demonstrates after reading. Orthographic development is a cumulative process for learning to read, with each skill building on the previously mastered skill. Fluency is an automatic recognition and accurate interpretation of text. Phonics is the ability to apply letter-sound relationships and letter patterns in order to accurately pronounce written words.

Subarea II—Development of Reading Comprehension

Vocabulary Development

Relationship Between Oral and Written Vocabulary Development and Reading Comprehension

The more words a reader knows, the more likely they are to understand what they are reading. There are strategies to develop vocabularies as well as move beyond single word recognition and into comprehension. While a good portion of vocabulary acquisition happens through passive learning, there are strategies to implement in a classroom to increase exposure to new words, build familiarity and confidence with known words, and, in turn, improve comprehension. Further, knowing a word is more than knowing the definition; it includes the ability to recognize the word, define it, and use it in written and spoken communication.

Because so much language learning happens indirectly, **extensive reading** is a useful strategy that improves fluency. Extensive reading means reading a lot at or below grade level. Providing more time for students to read like this in class is useful. Choosing texts that challenge students is also useful. When students are reading challenging or new texts, have them look ahead and skim for any unfamiliar words they can define. Additionally, teachers can have their students make their own vocabulary lists from readings and share those lists and word meanings with classmates.

Game playing in class is also a great way to encourage vocabulary and can include modified games like *Taboo*, *Pictionary,* or charades. Teachers can also work vocabulary in thematically, particularly as it relates to specific texts. For example, "Last Man Standing" is a game in which students stand in a circle and toss a ball to one another; the student with the ball must say a vocabulary word that fits into a particular theme. Students are "knocked out" of the game if they can't think of a new word or if they repeat one. The game continues until only one student is standing.

Reading aloud to students is also important, especially reading from texts that include new vocabulary words. Teachers can set aside 10 to 15 minutes during class time to have students hear new words in context from someone who reads fluently. When a new word is encountered, stop the reading while you define the word and point out any roots or affixes. After reading, discussion about the text and words should continue.

Post-reading discussion is an important strategy, one that can be included after individual reading. Having students re-tell or summarize what they've read with a partner and introducing any new vocabulary they ran across is an excellent method for encouraging vocabulary acquisition and comprehension.

Systematic, Non-contextual Vocabulary Strategies and Contextual Vocabulary Strategies

Non-contextual strategies for teaching vocabulary are those that rely on vocabulary lists and single word acquisition. Vocabulary taught in this manner should include new or unfamiliar words that are vital to understanding the content being read, words that will be useful in future reading, and words that

students are unlikely to encounter elsewhere. Non-contextual vocabulary is crucial, as students' exposure to certain words in context is fairly limited.

When introducing words in this manner, first go over pronunciation, as well as any roots or affixes, and then provide the definition. Definitions should use simple vocabulary that students already know. With younger learners, pictures that represent the word aid greater understanding. To deepen understanding of a word, provide an example of the word being used in different types of sentences. Then, check student understanding of the word by asking questions that use the word in a sentence. These should be simple yes or no questions so that teachers can gauge understanding. Finally, have students brainstorm lists of synonyms to demonstrate their knowledge of the word. By following this systematic progression, students not only learn and memorize the word, but they also gain a deeper understanding of its meaning and are then prepared to use the word in context. Individual word acquisition gives students a strong foundation on which to build contextual understanding.

In contrast, **contextual vocabulary** acquisition focuses on students learning the meaning of a word through inference and analysis of the text around it, or the context in which it appears. One of the best exercises for this is independent reading. However, it is worth noting that making vocabulary gains through independent reading requires a significant amount of time and may be best when given as homework. As noted above, because it takes many interactions with a new word to acquire vocabulary through reading and contextual understanding, reading independently at a level that is sufficiently challenging is important.

Contextual strategies rely on other learning in the area of vocabulary development, especially in regard to learning root words, affixes, and compound words. Any time a student can break down an individual word and define its parts, there is a greater chance they will be able to decode the meaning.

Modeling contextual decoding is an important part of instruction. Showing students how to look for contextual clues is best done through explanation and demonstration of the strategies. Context clues include definition, analogy, synonyms, examples, or antonyms that appear in the same sentence or in nearby sentences. You can show students a sentence with an unknown word and context clues to its meaning. Individual students should then attempt to define the word and say which context clue they used to discover the definition. Then, with partners or teams, students should discuss their answer. The group that is closest to the actual definition and gets the correct context clue wins. Activities like this reinforce the types of context clues.

English Literacy Development

English language literacy can be categorized into four basic stages:

1. Beginning

2. Early Intermediate

3. Intermediate

4. Early Advanced

Beginning Literacy

This stage is commonly referred to as **receptive language development**. Educators can encourage this stage in literacy development by providing the student with many opportunities to interact on a social

level with peers. Educators should also consider starting a personal dictionary, introducing word flashcards, and providing the student with opportunities to listen to a story read by another peer, or as a computer-based activity.

Early Intermediate Literacy

When a child begins to communicate to express a need or attempt to ask or respond to a question, the child is said to be at the early intermediate literacy stage. Educators should continue to build vocabulary knowledge and introduce activities that require the student to complete the endings of sentences, fill in the blanks, and describe the beginning or ending of familiar stories.

Intermediate Literacy

When a child begins to demonstrate comprehension of more complex vocabulary and abstract ideas, the child is advancing into the intermediate literacy stage. It is at this stage that children are able to challenge themselves to meet the classroom learning expectations and start to use their newly acquired literacy skills to read, write, listen, and speak. Educators may consider providing students with more advanced reading opportunities, such as partner-shared reading, silent reading, and choral reading.

Early Advanced Literacy

When a child is able to apply literacy skills to learn new information across many subjects, the child is progressing toward the early advanced literacy stage. The child can now tackle complex literacy tasks and confidently handle much more cognitively demanding material. To strengthen reading comprehension, educators should consider the introduction to word webs and semantic organizers. Book reports and class presentations, as well as continued opportunities to access a variety of reading material, will help to strengthen the child's newly acquired literacy skills.

Relationship Between Oral Vocabulary and Written Words

Acquiring vocabulary through speech is a vital component to identifying and understanding written words. If students possess the phonics skills, those skills can be transferred to the written word and then aid in identification.

Further, research suggests that if a student has heard a word before, they are more likely to read it correctly than if they are totally unfamiliar with it. Pronunciation and meaning create an expectation regarding what a word would look like when written, and so having heard a word before and understanding its meaning in conversation helps the reader. This is directly related to a student's understanding of the smaller parts of written words as well, again being able to connect the sound of a letter or a letter blend and vowels with written spelling. That means that when a student hears a new word, they are likely already considering how it might be spelled based on their existing knowledge. An exercise that practices this skill would be letting students hear a new word, having them predict how it is spelled, and then looking at and discussing its actual spelling. This allows students to identify sound and letter combinations that may help them read similar combinations and make those connections later. That said, it is worth considering that oral language skills should reflect listening and speaking skills, so having students pronounce new words aloud is recommended.

Much like reading, a student's knowledge of a word encountered in oral communication translates to a student's understanding of what the word means when written. If a student can read the word, sound it out, and pronounce it correctly, the connection can be made between the word they have heard and the written word.

Initially, oral communication will enhance a student's reading skills, recognition, and understanding, but eventually the relationship will become reciprocal, with reading skills enhancing oral communication skills.

Oral Language Development and Listening Comprehension

Oral language and presentation are also important in learning reading comprehension. Reviewing and identifying new and key vocabulary prior to reading the text help students understand the text more efficiently. Once students are familiar with new vocabulary words, they should be able to interpret the word in context of the reading, rather than reaching the word and skipping over the sentence or needing to stop and look up the word before continuing to read. This interrupts fluency as well as the understanding of the text. Previewing text and skimming pictures for younger students, or reviewing bold subtitles for older students, can benefit students' comprehension by helping to gain an idea of what the text may be about before reading. There are different ways to find a text's purpose using auditory and speech skills, some of which include summarizing with a peer or paraphrasing the text.

When students are paired together or placed in small groups, they can share and discuss elements of texts. Literature circles are like book clubs. These circles allow students to speak freely, create their own discussions, and form questions about the text. Teachers can provide literature circle booklets, which may contain response or discussion questions to enhance conversation within the group.

Common Sayings, Proverbs, and Idioms

Common sayings, proverbs, and idioms challenge a student's understanding of how to decode, because when the words are placed together in these structures, their meaning changes. That is, the phrase has a meaning that is different from what the words might traditionally mean independently. For example, a phrase like "hit the hay," which means "go to sleep," has a different meaning when translated literally. For this reason, sayings and idioms present a particular difficulty for students. However, they do present an opportunity for fun in the classroom, particularly with younger learners.

As these phrases and idioms can be difficult for early language learners to grasp, it's best to not introduce too many at once. One good way to keep them limited is to teach thematic idioms together. For example, you might choose to teach idioms or sayings related to color: *to have the blues, gray area, seeing red, out of the blue, caught red-handed,* and *tickled pink.* It may also be helpful and fun to use pictures, discuss the incorrect and implausible literal meaning, and have students guess at the phrase's actual meaning.

Using stories is another useful strategy. Introduce an idiom, such as *biting off more than I can chew,* and have students make up a story related to the idiom. *Don't count your chickens before they hatch* is another saying that lends itself to storytelling. Further, incorporating Shel Silverstein and *Amelia Bedelia* books, both of which play with idioms, can lead to discussions and further understanding. Pairing students' own storytelling with the storytelling of authors reinforces the fun of language learning, and it also demonstrates how easy it is to misunderstand language when we don't consider it in context.

Proverbs are similar to idioms in that they are phrases that go beyond the literal meaning. While students can work to decode the literal meaning, fables and other stories can introduce more complex proverbs. When introducing proverbs to students, start with those that have a literal meaning, such as *There's no place like home.* Students will likely know all the vocabulary, so they can start discussing the meaning of the phrase rather than decoding the meaning of words. From there, lessons can move into

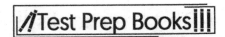

more intermediate proverbs, which may contain familiar vocabulary but require some interpretation. Proverbs such as *still waters run deep* use simple vocabulary, but they will require some discussion to discern the meaning. Early and intermediate proverbs can also be introduced through the use of fables. Aesop's Fables, for example, tell a story and then conclude with a proverb. Reading these together or even aloud, followed by guided discussions, will allow students to see the connections. Finally, more difficult proverbs that require some word decoding and interpretation, such as *He who pays the piper calls the tune*, may be introduced. Students may not know what a piper is and can have discussions about what the saying means.

The goal of teaching these types of phrases is to increase students' familiarity with them, through literature, frequent use in the classroom, and perhaps even student assignments that require them to use the phrases in their own writing or storytelling.

Foreign Words and Abbreviations Commonly Used in English

Another area where students may have difficulty in vocabulary acquisition is with foreign words commonly used in English. Because these words cannot be broken down with the strategies that students use to decode other words, it's important that they be discussed and introduced.

It may be worthwhile at this point to provide students with a bit of context regarding where the English language comes from and also how language travels around the world.

One strategy to use for these lessons is to categorize the words so students can begin to recognize them. Many students will recognize words from their own dinner tables. You may wish to further categorize by country, particularly with foods, as younger students may have more recognition. For example, teachers might ask them if they've had Mexican food, which introduces words like *burrito*, *taco*, *nacho*, *queso,* and *salsa.*

Starting with words that are familiar and easy to pronounce is key with younger learners. After discussing food words, you can then ask if they can think of other words that may come from Spanish. At this point, especially with younger learners, pictures come in handy, and the lesson might include *piñata* or *siesta*. Then move into words that are derived from Spanish, like *breeze*, *canyon*, *vanilla*, and *cockroach*.

The goal is to keep building on familiar words and categories; again, food is accessible to most students. Then, ask students to come up with other words from that language they might know. Finally, introduce words that are derived from the language in question rather than coming directly from that language. Each stage offers an opportunity to build on the previous stage.

Selecting Vocabulary Words

When selecting vocabulary words, it's important to first understand the different kinds of functional vocabularies we have. **Receptive vocabulary** words are those we recognize when we come across them in readings. **Expressive vocabulary** consists of the words we use when communicating. We can then further break down vocabularies into conversational, academic, and subject-specific. **Conversational words** are ones that students will be familiar with through everyday usage. **Academic words** are those that students will encounter while reading academic texts. **Subject-specific words** are those that students will likely encounter while studying specific subjects like math, art, or music.

60

Only when we understand these categories can we then make the best selections for vocabulary lessons. Conversational words can be left out of lessons because students will already be quite familiar with their meanings, usage, and spelling. Ideally, vocabulary words should be selected based on the following other criteria: importance, transferability, and usefulness for continued study.

Importance: How necessary is it that a student learn and know this word? If it is a word that a student will not likely encounter regularly, even in academic texts, it's likely not a good candidate. If a word is easily understood from context, it may not be one you wish to include in a vocabulary lesson, though teachers may want to discuss these words with students. If the word is important to a lesson being done concurrently in a different subject area, it may be important for a student to know it as well. Figuring out how relevant a word is to a student's current and future success, in reading and elsewhere, is an important first step in the selection process.

Transferability: Will this word be useful to students in other contexts? While choosing vocabulary words from chapter books and novels students are reading in ELA coursework, teachers will also want to evaluate whether those vocabulary words will be useful in other studies or outside the classroom. As a rule, words that students will rarely interact with or come across are often not the best choice for vocabulary lessons. There are academic word lists that teachers can use to determine which words meet this criterion.

Usefulness for continued study: Especially in early language acquisition, one of the best ways to determine whether a word is suitable is to ask whether it provides an opportunity for further growth and study. In other words, are there roots, suffixes, or prefixes that set students up for other vocabulary words with similar meanings? If, for example, *declaration* is a vocabulary word, it offers the opportunity to discuss the root, *clar,* which means *clear* and can set students up for other words like *clarity* or *clarification*. The same is true of prefixes like *pre-* as in *preview* or *bi-* as in *bipedal* or *bifocal*. The ultimate goal is choosing vocabulary words that serve double duty in teaching a student a new word and setting them up for future learning or vocabulary acquisition.

Unfamiliar Words Encountered in Connected Text

In connected text, words are not isolated; they appear in sentences. A strong reader is one who can decode and understand unfamiliar words when they are encountered in connected text. This goes beyond learning traditional vocabulary lists.

To ready students for connected text, it's crucial to teach them morphemes and the skills they need to break down and define words. Breaking a word down into its parts is one of the first strategies students can use to determine the meaning of a new word. Teachers can model the exercise with the entire class by putting a long word on the board and, with the students' help, breaking it down into parts that the students know until they can decode the word. This activity can then continue with students in small groups and a longer list of words until students can demonstrate this skill independently.

Students should also be taught to use contextual clues to help determine meaning. This first means helping them identify the contextual clues and then asking them to use the clues to clarify meaning. One way to teach the skill is to provide a list of vocabulary words and an incomplete text, and then have students fill in the blanks. Students will need to use the sentence around the blank to determine context and choose the appropriate word. This exercise need not be done with complex language; it can be done with words the students know or are working with in vocabulary lessons. One can also pull words from a text the students will learn later and incorporate these words as a vocabulary lesson. While the

61

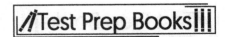

goal here isn't language acquisition as much as it is learning the concept of context itself, the two can be paired together.

Ideally, the best reading and word acquisition strategies incorporate additional skills that also build comprehension and learning. The final strategy here asks students to use other reference materials to help them learn the unfamiliar word. While teachers will need to offer instruction on the use of a thesaurus, dictionary, or glossary, both digital and nondigital, these reference materials are a valuable jumping off point for further learning. Students in pairs and small groups can be given a list of words; they can then use dictionaries to find multiple definitions, uses, and synonyms. This allows students to understand words through their use in other contexts as well as through other, similar words. Students then begin to build a collection of connected words to draw on in their own writing or apply in their reading.

Promoting Comprehension through Academic Language

One of the reasons English teachers focus on academic language is that it is cross curricular. **Academic language** is defined as the language and sentence structure used in academic texts and sometimes specific to content areas. Therefore, teaching academic language in the English classroom is crucial to student's success in other classes.

Many of the same strategies for working with other vocabulary can be applied here, provided texts used for instruction are varied and representative of other subject areas. In fact, vocabulary is one area where researchers suggest there be focus, as reading comprehension is the issue most students will face in more technical and subject-specific texts. For that reason, teachers should focus on choosing vocabulary words that students will encounter across the curriculum. Often, vocabulary lessons diminish throughout grade school, and this may be a pedagogical issue that needs to be addressed.

Once new vocabulary words have been introduced, students should then encounter them in multiple locations and through multiple modes of communication: reading, speaking, writing, and listening. Contextual interpretations should also be stressed, particularly as some words may have different meanings in different fields. Further, students should be required to do some etymological research, as learning about the derivation of words may contribute to understanding as well as acquisition of additional related words.

Multiple strategies exist to achieve these goals, including:

Alphaboxes: With this exercise, students use a chart with twenty-six boxes, one for each letter of the alphabet. In each box, they note key vocabulary words that start with that letter and are associated with the reading or the subject.

Word questioning: In this activity, students are given a word that will appear in the text they are reading. Then they must answer specific questions about the word, including what they think it means; an example from the text of how it is used (application); how it fits with other words on the topic (synthesis); where, when, and why the word might be used (knowledge); why the word is important to know (evaluation); and whether parts of the word are familiar (analysis). In being asked these questions, students learn quite a bit about the word and get many of the touch points they need to learn the word.

Linear array: This technique has students move from one vocabulary word in the text to another, using language from the text as well. In this way, they can draw connections between words, their meanings,

and related words. For example, a starting box might offer the word *egotistical*, followed by three empty boxes for the students to fill in on their way to the next vocabulary word, *indignity*.

Word sorts: This activity provides students with a list of the words or phrases they may encounter in the text they're reading. Working in teams or pairs, students sort the words into an order that tells a story or seems logical. The teacher will start to read the text and stop after a few minutes to allow students to re-sort their words. This will continue until the text is complete. At that point, students should put the words in the order the author of the text intended. Follow this with discussion about the words themselves and how they're related.

What students get from these activities is not only a stronger understanding of individual words, phrases, or language they may encounter, but also some of the strategies and tools needed to improve comprehension.

Reading Experiences in the Development of Academic Language and Vocabulary

One of the most effective ways for students to build their vocabularies is through reading. However, many students will not choose challenging texts. Because developing academic language skills is vital to a student's success in comprehending more complicated texts as they progress in their education, it is important that students be exposed to a wide variety of texts in the classroom. Varied texts are the best to ensure that students learn to analyze literature; understand complex ideas and research; and understand the vocabulary, structure, and syntax of academic language.

Most students do not come into contact with academic language in their everyday, non-school life. Therefore, in the English language classroom, teachers will want to make sure there are ample opportunities for reading. Students should be exposed to texts that cover a wide variety of subject areas to ensure that they encounter academic language. Lessons should include vocabulary instruction as well as inferencing and analysis. Vocabulary should then be repeated in instruction and used in students' own writing. Similarly, the structures and syntax of academic language in texts should be used as scaffolding for student writing.

Scaffolding, a technique that gradually increases the difficulty of a student's work and slowly asks for more independence from the student, includes many of the strategies we use to teach texts (vocabulary lessons, discussion, questioning), but it can also be used to transfer the academic structures and syntax to writing. Across a variety of texts, teachers can point out similar structures, such as transitions, and discuss how those words and the syntax of academic language helps create meaning and connections in a text. Language, syntax, and structures that students read eventually work their way into student writing and speech, developing their skills in that area.

Further, reading in the classroom should be extensive and intensive (varied). Extensive reading asks that students read daily at a level that is easy for them to understand. Typically, this would be at or just below grade level and something that they can read with significant fluency. One of the benefits of this kind of reading is that it re-exposes students to vocabulary they have seen before. Students rarely incorporate vocabulary into their own speech or writing without having had significant exposure to it. Extensive reading allows them to develop this skill.

Intensive reading, on the other hand, asks students to read closely. It is often difficult subject matter or difficult text that will require them to decode word meanings. Typically, these texts could be in subjects like science or social studies and would include new vocabulary. Intensive reading requires, sometimes,

rereading, analysis, discussion, and a lot of the comprehension strategies that force a student to stretch. Intensive reading materials should be short and of interest to readers in the student's age group. Intensive reading should also focus on concrete goals, such as vocabulary acquisition, learning a subject area, answering questions, or analyzing structures and syntax.

Academic Language and Vocabulary Knowledge and Skills in Individual Students

Academic language can be defined by vocabulary and by syntax. Academic vocabulary includes complex compound words, subject-specific words, and words defined as academic based on their usage in academic texts. There is concern about development of academic language and vocabulary among students, particularly as they enter more academically rigorous courses or grade levels. Research suggests that understanding and fluency in academic language is crucial to academic success and comprehension of advanced texts. However, many students fall short in this skill area.

A student's exposure to academic English is often limited to the educational setting. The English student's language at home, with peers, and in their communities is often informal; it is not structured like academic English. As a result, the opportunities for exposure to and practice using academic English are limited. Additionally, most curriculum does not focus on academic English itself nor are most students tested on their understanding of it. Because the makeup of academic language goes beyond simple vocabulary and includes phrasing as well as contextual understanding of complex ideas and sentences, improvement in these skills is based on student exposure to the increasing complexities in academic English. In fact, it is recommended that the path to this understanding begins in early education and extends through secondary education. Students who do not have this exposure risk falling behind, as do English language learners (ELLs) who are likely already struggling to catch up to peers when learning a non-native language.

The strategies to improve student success in academic English are comprehensive and ideally follow a student throughout the entire K–12 educational experience. Early education should focus on vocabulary development and a student's ability to complete a communication cycle, that is to listen, comprehend, and respond to a variety of conversation types from informative to exploratory discussions. Further, contextual clues to acquiring new language skills should be introduced at this time. As students progress in school, reading education should include learning to identify word structures so that students are able to break down new vocabulary into prefixes, suffixes, and root words. Additionally, discussions should focus on the connections between academic vocabulary and sentence structures and phrasing that are prevalent in academic texts.

While individual student success in this area will be impacted by exposure to formal English beyond the classroom as well as a student's native language knowledge, classroom support and integration of academic texts to regular classroom instruction is beneficial.

Imaginative and Literary Texts

Reading as a Process to Construct Meaning

Many early readers see reading as a passive activity. They see words as input and little more. As a result, they fail to actively engage with the text in a meaningful way. This impacts their comprehension and

64

absorption of the material. Strategic readers, on the other hand, have tools at their disposal to help them engage with the text and construct meaning. Their strategies include:

- **Inferencing**: Inferencing is making judgments or drawing conclusions from given information. Additionally, inferencing allows students to make predictions based on information given and what they already know.

- **Monitoring**: These anticipatory skills allow students to predict when text will be difficult to understand and prepare themselves for better comprehension. Specific monitoring skills include using diagrams, images, or graphs in the text; stopping when confused rather than just pressing forward; asking questions; looking up unfamiliar vocabulary; and soliciting extra help when needed.

- **Questioning**: Strategic readers ask questions as they read. These can range from questions about the text to questions for further study. As a student reads, have them keep a piece of paper nearby on which to write questions down.

- **Summarizing**: This is a crucial step in constructing meaning. To demonstrate that ideas are understood, a student must be able to summarize what they have read. For informational texts, this includes being able to identify the main ideas and supporting evidence. For fiction, students should be able to, at a minimum, identify plot points.

Each of these strategies should be explained in detail to students and then demonstrated or modeled. Students should then practice the strategy as they read texts in the classroom and for homework. Instructors may wish to isolate each of these strategies, leading with summarizing, to be sure students have a grasp of each before moving on to the next until students can confidently use them on their own.

Reading Comprehension and Analysis Skills for Reading Literature

Students should be allowed to monitor and assess themselves as they read. Graphic organizers and reading journals are great tools for self-monitoring. Many graphic organizers are preexisting and available for reproduction. Graphic organizers can also be student-generated, after students have had enough practice using them. Word webs can branch out details from one main idea. Sequencing graphic organizers can link the progression of main ideas from the story in chronological order. There are also cause and effect graphic organizers to recognize where in the story these elements occur. Fact and opinion graphic organizers can help students separate an author's bias from the facts in a text. Teachers can also create their own graphic organizers and display them as classroom posters or models for students to use as they create their own. Students should be encouraged to keep reading journals and document the objectives for each daily lesson, notes regarding the text, questions addressed by the student or teacher, predictions, and summaries of lessons or texts themselves. Teachers may direct the journaling by providing an objective for the journal for a given day, or teachers may give students several options to choose from.

Three Levels of Reading Comprehension

There are three levels of reading comprehension.

Literal: This stage is achieved when a student can recount what they have read, often recalling the basic details and order of events. This refers to information that is clearly explained or mentioned in the text.

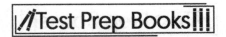

Inferential: Students achieving this level of comprehension can glean information that is implied in the text, but not stated explicitly. The student at this level can read the text and seek out information, gaps, and read between the lines to discover information provided through auxiliary details.

Evaluative: The final level of comprehension combines the first two and includes information taken from the student's world experience to draw conclusions and make judgements. Students are able to take what is in the text, provide additional information from their experiences, and provide new information of their own, based on the reading.

There are multiple strategies for promotion of reading comprehension that involve activities done before, during, and after reading. One excellent strategy is the **Directed Reading Thinking Activity (DRTA)**. Depending on their comprehension level, students make predictions and ask questions about a text, read the text, and then use evidence from the text to support or overturn their predictions and answer their questions. The first and last steps are often done as think-alouds, while the middle step can be accomplished through read-alouds. For more advanced readers, these can also be written assignments.

Before Reading

Prior to reading the text, teachers may wish to frame the reading by providing background information which may be relevant to understanding. This could also include any vocabulary the students may be unfamiliar with. This applies to readers at all three comprehension levels.

For students at the literal level: Teachers may also wish to discuss story structure (beginning, middle, and end) and some of the basic building blocks of a story such as setting, character, and theme. These learners may also wish to discuss the title, and perhaps make predictions about what the story will be about.

For students at the inferential level: Prior to the reading, teachers may wish to discuss symbolism, figurative language, conflict, and point of view. It may be worthwhile to do a refresher of some of the literal components of a story (plot, setting, etc.) as well. Additionally, providing questions in advance of reading will also require students to dig a bit deeper into the text and prepare them to look for the appropriate information. Questions should lead them to make inferences and to look for places in the story that lend themselves to interpretation.

For students at the evaluative level: Teachers may wish to offer a refresher of the first two levels and then offer potential historical or cultural contexts that provide necessary background to evaluate the text fully. For example, *The Book Thief* is best taught with the inclusion of history lessons on World War II and the Holocaust.

During Reading

During reading, at all levels, students should be reminded to use comprehension strategies, making notes regarding areas where there may be confusion. Also, for all levels, teachers should continue to ask questions throughout the reading that focus on the elements pertinent to the lesson or that will be discussed after the reading.

For students at the literal level: During reading, teachers should ask students to focus on important details and to summarize sections of the story, list characters, discuss the setting, and focus on literal understanding of the plot. What happened? Students should be able to summarize and reconstruct the events in order.

66

For inferential comprehension: During the reading, teachers should point out figurative language, passages that are open for interpretation, and ask questions about passages to model how strategic readers ask questions about inferences and meaning in a text.

For evaluative comprehension: Modeling opportunities for inference and evaluation is key here. It is important to point out these opportunities, offer interpretations and evaluations, and connect story elements to background or historical information. It can be appropriate here to offer examples and evaluations.

After Reading

For all three levels, post-reading discussion is paramount. This is an opportunity to discuss comprehension skills appropriate to student level. It's also an opportunity for a teacher to model the strategies students can use to extrapolate information from the text. Further, for the more advanced levels, modeling is key to students seeing, rather than being told, how inference and evaluation are successfully done. At those more advanced levels, it's also key to promote student exploration of ideas and interpretations, particularly those based on their personal experiences.

For literal comprehension: In addition to discussion, students should retell the story, recalling primary plot points and important information. Group or pair work here is possible as some students may remember different elements. These activities can be paired with further discussion about why these elements are important. Story maps or story frames are quite useful here as well.

For inferential comprehension: In addition to discussion, students can explore various ways to respond to the story itself via their own writing, changing the format such as from story to play, participating in debates as characters from the story, or other methods. At this level, students may also start to explore questioning the text by asking what the writer means by certain passages or why certain elements were included. Further opportunities to explore inferences about character, setting, or symbolism can be driven through questions that focus on those elements. Students should draw conclusions from information in the text rather than just repeating the text. In other words, asking what can be concluded based on given information is a useful strategy.

For evaluative comprehension: In addition to the strategies for inferential readers, evaluative readers should be asked to consider other stories, texts, or real-world events that connect to what they have read. From this, they can evaluate the connections and why they matter. Deeper analysis of the literary elements is also possible here, especially beginning to draw new conclusions about the text. Questions and discussion should be centered around making evaluations and supporting those conclusions with evidence and information from the text itself.

Reading Comprehension Strategies

Organizational/Explanatory Features

Using and understanding references is imperative in developing reading comprehension skills. Pre-teaching a lesson on understanding references can be helpful, or a teacher may even incorporate this skill into teaching some broader comprehension skills. Prior to teaching from the basal reader, or prior to each story in the basal reader, a teacher should address the table of contents at the beginning of the textbook. This teaches students to use the table of contents frequently and allows them to find parts of a story that they will be reading on their own. When teaching from nonfiction texts, such as social studies or science, instruction should be provided on using the index to identify and locate specific information to answer comprehension questions. Both nonfiction and fiction texts can be used to teach

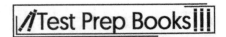

how to use the glossary to locate boldfaced and important vocabulary. It is often most beneficial to identify and teach new vocabulary prior to reading a piece, so that students gain a deeper understanding of the text as they read it for the first time.

Typographic Features

Understanding changes in the appearance of text will help students easily identify important information. Pointing out boldfaced words during reading instruction tells students these may be important words in the understanding of the text, and that new vocabulary may be present. Boldfacing or italics may help students identify when a thought or topic is changing or being brought to attention. Color-coding may be used when comparing or contrasting different parts of the text. During reading comprehension instruction time, it is important to point out when these changes occur. It is also helpful to try to find text of this nature to use in small group or whole group instruction. Text with these types of typographic features assist students on their path to reading comprehension.

Graphic Features

Graphics always help interpret a story or text. Younger learners rely on pictures to help tell the story, while older students use diagrams, maps, and charts to aid in understanding texts. Even for adults, graphic features assist with visualizing the text. Charts and diagrams help organize information into more clear and concise patterns. Maps help understand specific places and locations. Illustrations help visualize a fictional story. Furthermore, illustrations with captions help visualize nonfiction and fiction texts, particularly when paired with captions that provide an explanation of why the illustration is important.

Development of Literary Response Skills

A **literary response task** asks students to respond to, rather than summarize, a piece of literature they've read. This skill requires students to have literal comprehension skills. Once a student can effectively summarize a text, they can begin responding to it. One of the goals here is to have the students begin to interact, on a personal level, with the literature they're reading. Students can begin to ask questions about how a story relates to them and their world, setting the stage for more in depth analysis later.

One of the most important elements of teaching literary response skills is selecting appropriate content. Not every story or every piece of literature will resonate with students, so selecting one that will do that is vital. Students will connect to well-written stories with characters similar to their age and plots that relate to their own experiences. A text which offers them plenty of elements to respond to will result in better and more varied responses from students.

At earlier levels, responses can be as simple as asking students what the text makes them think about, how it makes them feel, how they relate to settings or characters, what things in their lives mimic plot points, and how they relate to other literal elements of the story. Working with plot diagrams, at this level, is useful as well. A good portion of this will be summary and response with the writing more divided than interwoven.

Once students have moved beyond literal comprehension skills, responding can also grow more complex. To demonstrate this skill and its application, teachers may wish to share book or movie reviews as they are good examples of where students may be exposed to literary response in their daily lives.

At more advanced levels, student responses should continue to grow more sophisticated offering analysis of the elements and offering new perspectives that may be related to other texts (fictional and nonfictional), historical events, or real-world experiences. Again, effective modeling is paramount here. The ability to draw these connections is demonstrative of advanced comprehension.

Development of Literary Analysis Skills

Literary analysis skills are the natural successor to a student's ability to understand and describe what they have read. It is an early stage in critical thinking, as it asks students to develop their own ideas and interpretations from a text. Making this step isn't always easy for students, especially those who are looking for information to be given to them rather than searching out meaning on their own and reading between the lines.

To engage in literary analysis, class discussion should begin with an overview of the text, including major plot points, to be sure all students understand the reading. Then discussion will move on to other elements, including areas of confusion and elements that lend themselves to interpretation. From this group discussion, students can build on their own ideas or develop new ones. Literary elements can be discussed in break-out groups. Keeping students focused on the end goal of analysis is key here, as many will be tempted to fall back on familiar skills of remembering, understanding, and summarizing. Remind students that analysis asks how or why rather than who or what. Analysis is more than identifying a moment in a story as a turning point. Students must ask why that moment is significant. If they suggest something in the text acts as a symbol for something larger, how can they support that claim? What other information in the text acts as evidence for that interpretation?

Moving students from summarizing to analyzing is a big step. One strategy is to have students read a story or part of a novel and then spend a few minutes writing down statements about what they have read. Next, have students identify which statements are facts or come directly from the text and which statements are analyses, judgments, or inferences they have made based on some of the facts. Once students have learned to differentiate between facts and inferences, class discussions can move into why the analytical statements might be true. Which statements of fact support the statements of analysis?

Literary analysis is one of the first steps to developing critical thinking skills and learning how to say what something means and why it's significant. Literary analysis skills enable students to move beyond the literal and to begin to ask questions about the things they read. This work is the essence of how to think.

Comprehension Strategies

There are several metacognitive strategies such as reviewing, rereading, visualizing, and self-monitoring that teach students to actively review how they think and the ways in which they learn. These skills are often incorporated into a variety of strategies designed to support and teach reading comprehension.

The first strategy that supports effective reading is previewing. This is not unlike book handling skills for younger readers. Students should familiarize themselves with the text, including any images, graphs, charts, diagrams, headings, and subheadings. They should also look at the length and any information they can glean prior to actually reading the text itself. This strategy should be modeled by the teacher, who goes through the text, points out these items, and discusses them with students. The teacher

should emphasize why these elements are significant, what they can reveal about the text, and how they can prepare us for reading.

Previewing is at the start of the **SQ3R method (Survey, Question, Read, Recite, and Review)**, which asks students to first survey the reading. Next, students are asked to formulate questions based on the preview. One effective strategy for this is to turn each of the headings or subheadings into a question. Students can then predict that the section will answer the question asked by the rephrased heading. The three *R*s are read, recite, and review. After reading, students recite by summarizing the main points of what they've read in a group. The review steps ask students to spend more time with the text, digging in more deeply after they have discussed the literal meaning. This can be done individually, in small groups, or as a full class discussion.

Another strategy is called **chunking**. This means breaking a long, complex text into chunks that are easier to deal with. Teachers can choose to break a text up by pages, sections, headings, or sub-headings. The smaller chunks allow students to identify unfamiliar vocabulary, dissect difficult sentences, and analyze details and ideas.

Close reading is another strategy that asks students to work independently and together in small groups to do a deep reading of a text. The first read-through, students read individually, making notes on the text. Next, the teacher reads the text out loud as students listen, mark unknown words, and note main ideas and details that encapsulate the meaning. Finally, the last reading is done in groups or with a partner; this reading includes questions that require students to apply outside knowledge or complete research to enhance their understanding. Rereading text multiple times is one of the most effective metacognitive skills for developing reading comprehension.

KWL charts are another strategy and involving principles similar to both of the previous methods. For a KWL chart, the *K* column is completed before students begin reading; it identifies what they already know about the topic. Students should brainstorm here and exhaust the knowledge they have about the topic, even if it seems slightly tangential. The *W* column asks what the student hopes to learn in the reading. This prepares them to read with a purpose. The *L* column is completed after the reading and includes what the student learned during the reading. This type of exercise helps students visualize and organize what they have read.

The **jigsaw strategy** allows students to learn from one another and master texts, so they can also teach others. For this strategy, students work in groups, with each group reading selections from the same text. Each group discusses their section, identifying main ideas, discussing difficult passages or sentences, and ensuring that they can then explain their section to another group. The students are then re-grouped with one student from each group forming a new group so that the new groups, with all the individual participants, will have "read" the entire text. Each student will summarize and share information about their independent sections so that by the end of the jigsaw, all the parts are put together to form a complete understanding of the text.

One final strategy is **think-pair-share**. This strategy asks students to complete a reading and consider, deeply, what they have read. The thinking portion asks them to write down their initial thoughts: any ideas the text brings up, questions they might have, and outside sources it brings up. Then students break into pairs and discuss their ideas with one another. Finally, each pair then shares with the class at least one idea they discussed. Having students evaluate their initial thoughts both by themselves and with classmates is an excellent method of self-monitoring that can help each individual student gain a

better understanding of what they understood and what they did not understand when reading the text.

These strategies ask students to engage with the text in multiple ways and throughout the entire process, from pre-reading to reading and then beyond. Comprehension is a process that extends beyond completion of the text, and these strategies seek to teach that to students.

Oral Language Activities

When students are paired together or placed in small groups, they can share and discuss elements of texts. Literature circles are like book clubs. These circles allow students to speak freely, create their own discussions, and form questions about the text. Teachers can provide literature circle booklets, which may contain response or discussion questions to enhance conversation within the group.

Role of Reading Fluency in Facilitating Comprehension

Fluency and comprehension rely on one another. The more fluent a reader, the more that reader comprehends. Similarly, the better a student understands words, their meanings, and the ways they connect, the more fluent their reading is. In fact, students who score low on fluency also score low on comprehension.

Fluency is not all about speed. Before a student can read quickly, they must read accurately. Students must be familiar with the vocabulary and not run into many words that are unfamiliar, multi-syllabic, or require decoding. This seems to be the crux of research regarding fluency and comprehension, that students who read fluently free up capacity to shift thinking to comprehension rather than focusing on vocabulary and unknown words, which naturally slow a reader down.

Therefore, the first goal of reading for fluency and comprehension is to develop a student's vocabulary. While vocabulary lessons here are important, particularly as related to new and unfamiliar words, one of the better strategies is to strengthen existing vocabularies through efforts such as extensive reading. In other words, it is vital to incorporate a significant amount reading at a level that is easy for a student, introduces no new words or concepts, and simply allows a student to strengthen existing vocabulary skills.

Further, students should be introduced to readings across subject areas as these areas are the first places they may encounter more complex subject matters. The focus is on strengthening existing vocabulary to build fluency.

The final step is to work on vocabulary strategies that allow students to decipher meanings through morphological awareness. This means breaking words down into smaller units, such as affixes or words they may know. Contextual meaning should also be introduced here, but even that relies on a student's understanding of most of the vocabulary introduced.

The goal of fluency is to increase a student's capacity for reading comprehension. Fluency also increases a student's understanding of language itself. Reading speed and the ability to comprehend words lead to an increased ability to understand tone and mood. Further, students can read with the rhythm of the intended language, which is particularly important in reading literature and poetry.

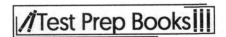

Writing Activities that Reinforce Comprehension

Use of **writing activities** to promote text understanding is helpful for comprehension of expository and informational texts along with literary and imaginative texts. Writing activities that coordinate with daily skills addressed in the classroom enhance reading comprehension, help demonstrate students' understanding, and also serve as great notes for future use and for class discussions. Composition notebooks can be used as literary response journals. Teachers can also create booklets with questions that are pre-printed inside. These journals provide students with the opportunity to record their thoughts, ideas, or reflections about texts. Teachers may respond to students' journal entries or simply use them as a guide for future discussions. Otherwise, teachers can post discussion questions or the daily journal topic on a projector or board. Daily activity ideas include summaries of the day's reading, discussion questions, comprehension questions, and character analyses. Along with reading journals and graphic organizers, taking organized notes can help students build comprehension skills. Students who write what they learn actually achieve higher test scores than those who do not. Therefore, students should summarize what they have read in notes or outlines. Note taking will help students respond to questions; it will be easier to locate important information from their own notes and outlines rather than a whole text. The written text also promotes memory of the information.

Additionally, compare and contrast writing activities can help students engage with various texts at a deeper level by asking why questions as well as what questions. Exercises might include discussions of different versions of a story or various treatments of a theme across a selection of texts and genres, with an emphasis on asking why the differences are important and what the authors intend to show to their readers.

Reading Comprehension Skills and Strategies of Individual Students

Students all have their own skills and experiences. It's the role of the teacher to meet these students where they are and use strategies that speak to their individual talents and needs. Regardless of the student's needs, some of the primary strategies for reading comprehension will assist them all. Some of these reading strategies involve pre-reading, which is preparing for a text by discussing the topic and the title, predicting what the text might be about, discussing vocabulary, and scanning the text itself. Some reading strategies are done during the reading: discussing interpretations or symbols, pointing out difficult words and contextual clues, and asking questions. Post-reading activities include discussions, question and answers, think-pair-share, and other activities that match stronger readers in groups or pairs with readers who would benefit from a partner.

Students who come from homes where English is not the primary spoken language may have reading comprehension issues, even if English is the student's first language. Similarly, homes where academic language is not part of everyday conversation, or where reading behaviors are not modeled and books are not present, may need to do extra work to catch up to peers who have these benefits. All these situations can contribute to issues with reading fluency and comprehension based on lack of exposure to spoken vocabulary. A reader's exposure to spoken language, environmental print, and early experiences with book handling skills may impact them later in school, particularly with reading. To work with these students, segmentation in the classroom is useful. **Segmentation** is breaking students into groups that appropriately reflect their skill levels, allowing teaching to focus on shared areas of weakness. Texts can be chosen to match the students' level of ability; the ideal text is one that pushes students but is not so challenging that it's discouraging. Further, segmentation allows students who are

having more success in comprehension to discuss more complex ideas and work with more difficult texts.

For vocabulary acquisition, students who have reading comprehension issues would benefit from images paired with vocabulary words as well as environmental print used in the classroom to increase their exposure to language. These students may also need instructors to check in more frequently on comprehension, to ask more questions, and to work, at times, with peers who may be stronger readers. Breaking reading into smaller chunks will also help these readers, as large sections of text may be overwhelming. Finally, when moving from reading to written text, framing sentences will work well for them. "Fill-in-the-blank" exercises help them understand structure as well as vocabulary.

In addition to ELLs and other students for whom language exposure has been limited, there are other types of learners. It has been claimed that learning styles are a myth, but it is still ideal for teachers to use multiple instruction styles.

For **kinesthetic learners**, think activities that will get students moving. This can include games like rhyming word hopscotch: students can't move to the next square on the floor until they read a word. There are also sight word relay races, in which students move from cone to cone but can only progress once they have read the word. If space is available, story walks can be constructed; in this activity, students follow a path and read a story as they go along. At the end, they must bounce a ball in different squares, revealing key elements of the story such as title, characters, and plot points. A story work can be done individually or in groups. Additionally, activities can involve flashcards, building blocks, and other objects that students must manipulate to create sentences and stories.

For **auditory learners**, read-aloud opportunities and audiobooks are fantastic options. These students can further practice by retelling the story or what they've read. In addition to texts being listened to, simply playing soft instrumental music while doing independent reading may be very helpful.

For **visual learners**, using images associated with stories and vocabulary is very helpful. Once students advance beyond pictures, using graphic organizers is a great strategy. During reading, teaching students to use highlighters helps them visualize and remember important information. After reading, there are many options for mapping out readings, including plot maps, story charts, vocabulary charts, and other **graphic organizers**. Laying out text information in visual format helps these learners organize their thoughts, and it may also help with retention.

One reason assessment is useful in the classroom is that it allows a teacher to determine which strategies are working. While segmenting students is useful, there is still a variety of students in those segments who may find some strategies more useful than others. Therefore, introducing a variety of methods and strategies is important.

Informational and Expository Texts

Reading Comprehension and Analysis Skills for Reading Informational Text

It is important for students to be exposed to a variety of texts, reading materials, and resources. To become well-rounded readers, teachers should provide students with expository texts in addition to the classroom textbooks. Key characteristics of informational and expository texts include informative facts about a specific topic. Since these are nonfiction texts, diagrams or other graphic aids may be used to assist in understanding the text. Other forms of informational text include news articles, research

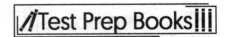

journals, educational magazines with informational text, and websites. These texts can be used in small groups or can be introduced in whole group instruction, and then further explored in small **intervention groups**. Intervention groups are useful because they allow small groups of students to focus more intently on a particular problem, area of instruction, or topic than can be achieved by the group as a whole. They can be used both to address particular issues experienced by readers who are less fluent and to allow more advanced students to explore a particular topic of interest in greater depth.

Fact-based understanding and the use of textual evidence is imperative in expository and informational texts. Students should be able to compare and contrast two different texts and identify problems and solutions as well as cause and effect. Graphic organizers arranged chronologically can help students take notes when covering nonfiction texts. Students need to have the correct order of events in a nonfiction piece in order to identify the cause of an event, as well as the effect it had on problems and solutions. At times, students may need to compare and contrast two texts to identify the similarity of facts, the differences in reported facts, or note any bias from the author. Using knowledge of writing standards and instruction can aid students' understanding of informational text. When comprehending an informative text's objective, students should utilize their prior knowledge of the topic, prior writing assignments, and concluding sentences in the text. This is another example of how reading comprehension and writing go hand-in-hand in the learning process, and how writing and language become important to student comprehension.

Levels of Reading Comprehension for Informational/Expository Texts

There are three levels of reading comprehension:

The **literal level** means understanding the events or explicit meaning of a text. A student who reads a chapter on trees and is then able to accurately answer questions about the definition of *evergreen* and *deciduous* trees has literal comprehension of the chapter. Students at the literal level can answer factual questions and summarize the text.

The **inferential level** of comprehension is the ability to read between the lines of a text and make generalizations and educated guesses. A student with inferential comprehension could read a book about mammals and then use the criteria in that book to identify that dogs and cats are mammals. Students at the inferential level are able to answer questions about what will happen next in a book and how the information in the text relates to their knowledge and experience.

The **evaluative level** refers to the ability to read critically and evaluate the quality of information instead of simply absorbing it. An evaluative reader could read an essay and then argue that the author's claims are invalid because their logic is flawed. Students at this level of comprehension can answer questions such as "Is this text accurate?" and "Is the author biased?"

Comprehension levels are not universal. Students will be at different levels for different texts. Comprehension is especially dependent on the level of text complexity. For instance, a middle school student with good reading skills would have high comprehension if he or she was reading the class's science textbook but low comprehension if asked to read a college textbook about the same material. Additionally, students' comprehension will vary based on the subject matter. A student who has a great deal of background knowledge in history but little in science will be able to reach higher comprehension levels in history.

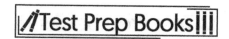

There are a number of strategies for improving reading comprehension at all three levels:

At any level, **guiding questions**, or questions teachers give to students before they read the text, are a great way to help students engage with the text. Students then use the questions to stay on track while they read. For example, consider a teacher who assigns their students a lesson about the life cycle of moths. The teacher could aid literal comprehension by asking questions such as "How many stages are in the moth life cycle?" To help students move on to inferential comprehension, questions such as "At what stage would you predict that moths are most vulnerable to predators?" would be useful. Finally, the teacher could use questions such as "Do you think the author's observations about moths are accurate?" to help students build evaluative comprehension.

Teachers can use summarizing exercises to help students gain literal and inferential comprehension. At the literal level, **summarizing** simply means describing the facts in the text (e.g., writing down the differences between vascular and nonvascular plants). At the inferential level, students can begin to make more complex summaries by including ideas that are not stated outright in the text (e.g., making up their own examples instead of using the ones given in the text). Summary assignments are also flexible, and teachers can tailor them to meet their students' needs and abilities. Young students can give oral summaries or write them collaboratively with the teacher, and more advanced students can work independently or in small groups.

Modeling can help students learn reading comprehension techniques and is particularly useful for teaching more advanced skills such as critical thinking. For example, a teacher could show the class how to evaluate the author's argument by writing their thought process on the board.

Close Reading of Informational/Expository Texts

There are numerous strategies that help students read closely and reach an evaluative understanding of informational texts.

The ability to evaluate logical arguments is one of the most important skills readers can learn because it enables them to distinguish valid arguments from claims that are misguided. Teachers can help students learn to evaluate logic by modeling their own thought processes. It can also be helpful to have students write out the author's claims in order and then look for faulty logic in the progression of claims. For instance, a student might recognize that an author is making a logical error by claiming that, because monkeys enjoy looking in mirrors, monkeys must be concerned about their appearance. A monkey could enjoy mirrors for any number of other reasons and might not even recognize that the animal in the mirror is itself.

Along with evaluating logical processes, students should be able to analyze the author's use of evidence by identifying the facts that undergird a text's argument and analyzing whether these pieces of support are valid. For example, a teacher might guide students to realize that, although the author of a scientific piece has factual support for the majority of their claims, they make one claim without referencing any facts to back it up. The students could then discuss whether there is evidence for or against the claim and experiment with both strengthening the author's flawed argument and attacking it. Teaching students to evaluate the use of evidence is also useful because it shows them how to correctly support their own arguments in discussions, debates, and essays.

Teachers should also help students learn to recognize the author's point of view and compare different descriptions of the same event or subject. Understanding these aspects of the text allows students to

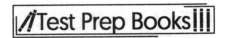
recognize bias and understand that people with different viewpoints can offer contrasting perspectives on the same topic, even if they are trying to be logical and truthful. For instance, a teacher might have students read two descriptions of life in ancient Egypt, one by an Egyptian author and one by a Greek historian. The students could then look for similarities and differences in the two accounts, identify elements of bias in both authors' perspectives, and compare their assumptions.

Students need to be able to tell the difference between facts and beliefs. This skill will enable them to recognize pieces of evidence that are not factual and to distinguish between claims an author is trying to prove and elements the author is simply voicing as a personal opinion. One way teachers can help students grasp this distinction is by having them discuss a topic with a partner and write down facts and opinions that arise during the discussion.

Reading Strategies for Different Texts and Purposes

There are three basic purposes for texts: to entertain, to inform, and to persuade. Of course, there is some overlap between these categories. A good children's book will often attempt to entertain as well as teach by presenting interesting stories and examples. However, most texts have a clearly defined primary purpose. For instance, even if a book about the life cycle of butterflies is entertaining, its primary purpose is to teach.

The way in which students should approach a text depends on its purpose. When reading texts that are intended solely for entertainment, students do not need to memorize facts or analyze arguments. Instead, they can focus on enjoying the content and style of the work. For example, a student reading a book of riddles is concerned with enjoying and trying to guess the riddles, not memorizing their details.

Informational texts present facts, and the students' primary concern is to learn those facts. A student who is reading about World War I, for instance, should be trying to memorize facts, such as the cause of the war, the countries involved, and the timeline of the war's events.

Reading persuasive texts requires more critical thinking than the other two types because readers need to evaluate the argument and decide whether it is valid instead of simply absorbing information. Students should understand the supporting evidence the author is using; however, they need to focus on the author's logic just as much as the facts themselves. For example, consider a student who is reading a paper that argues that calculus should not be taught in high school because it is irrelevant to everyday life. This student certainly needs to consider the author's evidence, but he or she should also try to think of facts the author has left out. For example, the author may have omitted the information that learning calculus sharpens the mind and allows students to determine whether they are suited for careers in math or science.

Students do not always need to understand every element of a text. To avoid wasting time learning information they do not need to understand, they need to know how to adjust their reading speed and attention level to suit various reading goals.

There are numerous reasons to read a text, and each purpose has unique comprehension strategies. Reading for complete comprehension of the text is the most common purpose for students in school. For this type of reading, annotating the text and taking notes are great comprehension strategies. Students can look up and define words that confuse them, highlight major points, and write down questions they have about the text. Teachers can tailor note-taking and annotation to suit the needs of children with different levels of maturity. For example, a teacher could ask younger students to simply

76

underline parts of the text they believe are important. Older students can complete more complicated activities, such as making explanatory notes on parts that confuse them and bringing discussion questions to class. Guiding questions can be useful to keep students of any age on track with their note-taking.

Reading a text to compare it with another text is similar to reading for complete comprehension, and although annotations and notes are certainly helpful, the goal of this type of reading is more focused. Instead of examining the piece as an independent work, students are looking for similarities and differences between it and the other text. Students should learn to hone in on these factors. Cross-referencing the two texts can be a helpful exercise. For instance, students could underline a point in the text and write down the page number of the section in the other text to which it correlates.

Reading to locate or learn specific facts does not demand the same attention to detail and complete comprehension as most other reading purposes. A student who is looking over a text to find out whether it is relevant to an essay he or she is writing does not need a deep understanding of the piece. Alternatively, a student might want to gain a basic understanding of the French Revolution because it was mentioned in an assigned reading. Rather than a thorough understanding of the text, all this student needs is an overview of the material so he or she can understand the assigned reading. The best strategy for this type of reading is *skimming*. **Skimming** is the process of reading quickly and looking for keywords instead of trying to understand the complete text. Because some students may feel guilty for this kind of "lazy" reading, it is important that teachers introduce it as a valid strategy for some reading contexts.

In order for students to know when to use which strategy, it is important that they learn to ask themselves what kind of reading they are doing and set comprehension goals before they begin reading. For example, a student reading for complete comprehension could set the goal "When I have finished this text, I will be able to give a complete summary of it from my notes." A student reading to locate a fact, on the other hand, might set a goal as simple as "I will find out whether this text mentions frogs." Setting goals helps students know which strategies to use and also gives them a way to objectively evaluate whether they have read the text successfully. If they have not fully met their goals, they can go back and read the sections of the text they did not grasp.

Comprehension Strategies to Support Effective Reading

Just as guiding questions from the teacher can keep students on track while they read, teaching students to invent their own questions and answers can improve their understanding of the material. At its simplest, **self-questioning** can mean students asking themselves questions as they read and then seeking the answers (e.g., "What does the author mean by this word?"). For a more involved exercise, you might ask students to write down three questions and answers about the text. Beginning students can focus on factual questions, such as "What is the difference between a camel and a dromedary?" However, you can ask more advanced students to try to invent more complicated questions, such as "Could the author's data on camel and dromedary behavior be skewed by the fact that there are far more dromedaries than camels?" Teachers can turn these questions into class activities by having students quiz each other on facts or facilitating discussions based on students' questions.

Paraphrasing allows students to gain new understanding of the text by putting it in their own words. By eliminating the words and constructions of which children have only a shaky grasp, paraphrasing ensures that they understand every part of the text. For example, a student might read, "Bears are omnivores, consuming both vegetation and meat," and paraphrase it into something like "Bears eat

other animals, but they also eat fruits and vegetables. The fact that they eat both types of food means they are omnivores." One way to have students paraphrase is by asking them to pretend they are teaching the subject to another student.

Rereading is also a valuable strategy because it allows students to pick up information they missed during their initial reading. Students can reread the whole text or just a part, depending on the difficulty of the piece and how much information they gained from reading it the first time. It is particularly useful to teach students to evaluate their understanding of a text after reading it and determine whether they should reread to address gaps in their knowledge; this type of self-monitoring is a metacognitive skill that is extremely important for effective reading.

Visualization helps internalize meaning by translating into imagery. For instance, you might practice auditory comprehension with young students by reading them a book and having them draw the story. Visualization is especially helpful for children who are visual learners because it teaches them to make up and learn from their own images when they are not provided in the text.

Oral Language Activities to Promote Comprehension

Although teachers can always invent their own activities for their classrooms, there are a number of exercises that are useful in many situations. **Discussions** are a way for students to practice summarizing and forming arguments in an informal setting. Teachers can guide the discussion to meet the needs of the students and promote the comprehension skills they need to practice. For example, a teacher whose students struggle with literal comprehension could ask them to go around the circle and share one interesting fact they learned from the reading. Because students will pick different facts, this exercise would allow them to review points they might have missed while reading the text. Alternatively, a teacher whose students are building inferential and evaluative comprehension could ask them to bring questions and/or observations about the text. The students could then work collaboratively to answer each other's questions and talk about the significance of the observations.

Debates are more formal than discussions. Instead of simply allowing the students to talk, the teacher breaks students into teams and asks them to argue about a point. For instance, a teacher could separate students into two teams—one arguing that the bombing of Japan during World War II was justified and the other arguing that it was unjust. The relative formality of debates encourages students to prepare in advance and often motivates them to put more effort into comprehension than they normally would.

Retelling means summarizing orally in a group setting. Students can retell the text individually or as a group. A teacher might ask for a volunteer to retell what happened in the first chapter of a text or conduct a group retelling exercise by seating the students in a circle and asking them to go around the circle with the first student beginning to summarize and each additional student beginning to retell at the point where the previous student left off. This type of group exercise works best when the students are either retelling a simple story or are able to refer to the notes they made on a more complex text.

Acting out the text allows students to retell a piece in a creative way. For example, a teacher whose class is studying the Magna Carta could assign parts and ask students to ad-lib a discussion between King John and his officials. Acting is a great way to help students fully engage with the text, and it can encourage students who have trouble speaking up in class to share their thoughts in a fun way.

Role of Reading Fluency in Informational/Expository Texts

Reading fluency is a student's ability to recognize words automatically. **Non-automatic reading** means consciously recognizing each letter or word and then putting them together; **automatic reading** means reading a word through subconscious processes, which makes reading seem effortless. For instance, you have probably not been sounding out every word in this book. Rather, your reading processes are so subconscious that you grasp the words as a whole. It is important to note that automatic reading is not synonymous with memorization of sight words. Students who read words phonetically can reach complete automatic fluency because the phonetic recognition occurs subconsciously. Fluent readers typically only read consciously when they are sounding out a new word.

Reading fluency plays a central role in students' ability to comprehend what they read. Students who read fluently (or automatically) have higher comprehension because they are able to put their effort into understanding the text instead of using up all their energy to read it. Reading fluency also makes reading far more enjoyable because students are able to absorb the text easily instead of struggling to read each word. This enjoyment motivates students to read the whole text instead of skipping words or sections and builds a positive attitude toward reading that inspires them to strive for comprehension.

Fluency is not the only factor that contributes to reading comprehension. Some students are able to read automatically but do not have the language skills or background knowledge necessary to reach an appropriate level of comprehension. For example, a student who struggles with vocabulary will have difficulty understanding texts, even if he or she can read them. Conditions such as attention deficit disorder (ADD) and attention deficit hyperactive disorder (ADHD) can also impact comprehension by making it difficult for students to concentrate. In addition, family and personality factors can influence students' comprehension. Some students' families do not encourage them to apply themselves at school, and other students struggle with motivation.

If you want to see whether a student's reading fluency is affecting their comprehension, you can read aloud to the student and test their auditory comprehension. A student with high auditory but poor written comprehension is likely suffering from poor reading fluency. A student who scores poorly in both areas, however, probably struggles because of a lack of language skills, attention problems, or other issues.

Writing Activities to Promote Comprehension

There are numerous writing activities that can improve your students' comprehension. As mentioned previously, summarization is an excellent way to build reading comprehension at all levels. Summaries can be as simple as descriptions of the factual events in a text or as complex as a rearrangement of the facts. Teachers can also use two-part assignments or book reports, in which the students write both a summary of the text and a response that includes their own opinions and arguments.

Teaching students to take notes and make outlines of the text can also improve comprehension. When teaching these skills, it may be helpful to have students hand in their notes and outlines so teachers can offer pointers on ways to improve. Teachers can help students build note-taking and outlining skills by making collaborative notes and outlines in class.

Semantic maps, which visually organize information by dividing it into types and subtypes, can also be useful. For example, a semantic map of mammals might divide "mammals" into the subtypes "aquatic" and "land dwelling." It could then divide the subtype "aquatic" into "seals" and "whales." Semantic

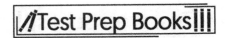

mapping, such as the following, allows students to organize complicated information in a way that is simple and easy to access.

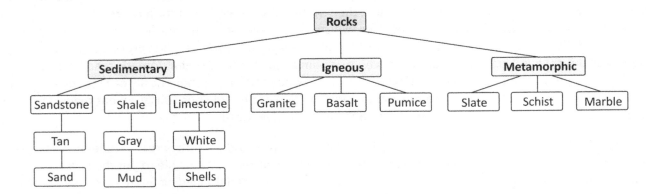

Teachers can also ask students to write their own questions and answers about the text. For example, you can ask them to pretend they are writing a test on the material they have just read. They can invent exam questions and then write answers to these questions. This type of exercise encourages students to perform close reading and seek out the answers to their own questions about the text. You can also motivate students to take this activity seriously by using some of the best student-invented questions on the actual class exam.

Persuasive essays can be a valuable way of helping more advanced students build comprehension. These assignments promote high-level comprehension skills, particularly evaluative comprehension, by demanding that students use textual evidence to construct their own arguments. For example, a teacher could ask students who have read a text about the different forms of government to write a persuasive essay on which form is the best. This assignment would aid comprehension because it urges students to understand what government terms are as well as read closely and form opinions about the strengths and weaknesses of each form.

Text Structures

Text structures are common ways of presenting information. Because these methods of organization are fairly standardized, they can help students predict what kind of information they will encounter and enhance their comprehension of the material.

There are five common ways to structure a text: descriptive, chronologically, problem/solution structure, cause and effect structure, and comparison/contrast structure.

Descriptive text structures relate information about an idea, fact, or thing. For instance, a descriptive text about grasshoppers would provide information about grasshoppers' anatomy, habits, etc. Descriptive texts are often divided into sections about different topics. The grasshopper book might have separate sections on subjects such as life cycle, diet, and habitat. Although the order in which these broad headings occur is not usually important, remembering the topical headings can help students organize the information in their minds and assess their understanding of it. For example, a student who remembers that there was a heading about habitat but does not remember any facts about the subject knows that he or she has missed some information and should reread the section.

Chronological text structures tell events in the order in which they occurred. A chronological book about the American Revolution, for instance, might begin with the Boston Tea Party, move on to the Declaration of Independence, and then go on to discuss important battles in order. Chronologically structured texts are the opposite of descriptive texts in that the order of information is just as important as the information itself. If a student thinks the Boston Tea Party happened after the American Revolution was over, he or she will miss a critical fact about the buildup to the war. When studying chronological texts, students may benefit from making timelines with dates to help them remember the information in the correct order.

The **problem/solution structure** is a way of examining the importance of an issue and presenting a way (or multiple ways) to resolve it. For example, an author who discusses the problem of deforestation and then presents methods of reducing humans' impact on the environment is using a problem/solution structure. When reading this type of text, students should analyze the solution the author proposes and evaluate its potential to solve the problem. If the author presents several alternative solutions, students should be prepared to compare them and determine their strengths and weaknesses.

A **cause-and-effect structure** shows the relationship between two factors. For instance, a passage that argues that people work less efficiently when they are unhappy is pointing out a cause-and-effect relationship between unhappiness (the cause) and inefficient work (the effect). Sometimes, students confuse the cause with the effect and arrive at false conclusions, such as "Ineffective work causes unhappiness." To avoid this trap, students should learn to look for words such as "because" and "since," as these words indicate which element is the catalyst and which is the result.

The **comparison/contrast structure** juxtaposes two ideas or facts. A compare/contrast essay on female novelists, for example, might discuss the similarities and differences between Jane Austen and Charlotte Brontë. The piece would probably pick themes addressed by both authors and then compare how the authors treat these topics. When reading this type of text, students might want to keep a list of similarities and differences.

Often, authors use different text structures in different parts of the same work. For instance, a geology book that is generally structured as a descriptive text might include sections that examine the cause-and-effect relationship between floods and rock formations, compare/contrast sections on different types of rock, and provide chronological explanations of how rocks are formed. Students should be able to recognize the shift between different text structures so they know what to expect from the passage and can understand the author's message.

Text Features, Graphic Features, and Reference Materials

Text Features

Text features are parts of a text that are outside the main text. For example, a book's table of contents is not part of the main text. Instead, it helps readers orient themselves and use the text more effectively. Two other common text features include the following:

An **index** provides keywords and corresponding page numbers to help readers locate information in a text. For example, a book on insects would have index entries such as "ant," "bee," and "beetle." An index differs from a table in contents because it arranges topics alphabetically instead of by the order in which they appear, and therefore makes it easier for readers to find specific information. Additionally, indexes are often more detailed than tables of contents. A table of contents might only provide general topics, such as "bee," but an index would break those topics down into subtopics, such as "honeybee"

and "bumble bee." Indexes can help students conduct research for their assignments and review information they missed during the initial reading.

Glossaries are like miniature dictionaries. They define potentially confusing words contained in the text. Whereas chemistry text might define subject-specific words such as "isotope," a history book might explain archaic words such as "bodkin." Teaching students to use glossaries helps them improve their comprehension.

Graphic Features

Graphic features are images that appear in the text. There are four common types of graphic features: illustrations, charts, maps, and timelines.

Illustrations are pictures that help students understand a text by representing it visually. A verbal description of an animal that most students have never seen, such as a capibara, would probably leave students with a general idea of what the animal looks like. However, a picture of a capibara would allow them to completely understand the animal's appearance. Additionally, illustrations can help students grasp complicated movements, understand new shapes, and summarize information.

Charts present factual or numeric information graphically. For example, a pie chart represents percentages and groups, such as percentages of brown-, blue-, green-, and gray-eyed people in the United States. Charts are a great way for students to quickly compare numbers and facts. Because they can organize large amounts of information, they are especially useful when the facts are complicated. Here are several examples of charts:

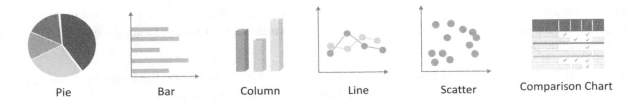

| Pie | Bar | Column | Line | Scatter | Comparison Chart |

Maps are a great way to represent space and movement. For instance, a map of the world highlighting the areas Britain controlled in the nineteenth century could help students understand the extent of British imperialism. Alternatively, a map with arrows detailing Magellan's path to circumnavigate the globe would allow students to grasp his route.

Timelines help students remember an order of events by mapping them out in chronological order. A timeline of the English Civil War, for example, could begin with the rebellion in Scotland, include important battles and other events, and end with Charles I being executed and Oliver Cromwell assuming power.

Along with helping students grasp chronological order, timelines, such as the following, act as summaries of essential information.

1960s Timeline

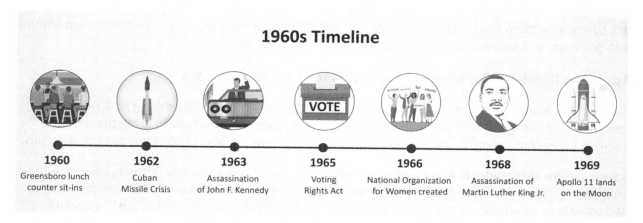

1960	1962	1963	1965	1966	1968	1969
Greensboro lunch counter sit-ins	Cuban Missile Crisis	Assassination of John F. Kennedy	Voting Rights Act	National Organization for Women created	Assassination of Martin Luther King Jr.	Apollo 11 lands on the Moon

Reference Materials

Reference materials are sources that summarize or provide background information about the text the students are studying. For instance, students who are studying Medieval jousts could use an encyclopedia to look up lances, learning more about the weapons through the information and pictures provided. Sometimes teachers create their own reference materials; a teacher could give students who are reading a history book a summary of important events and dates. Teachers can prepare students to work with reference materials by exposing them to the wide variety of sources available (dictionaries, encyclopedias, bibliographies, etc.) and teaching them the research skills they need to use such resources effectively.

Application of Comprehension Strategies to Electronic Texts

There is some evidence that suggests people have more trouble comprehending text when they read it on a digital platform, particularly if the text is lengthy or complicated. But because students need to learn how to read electronic texts effectively, teachers should make an effort to incorporate them into the lessons and teach the skills needed to understand information in this potentially confusing medium. Although most comprehension strategies transfer from print to electronic texts without changing at all, there are a few differences between the mediums.

Because students typically need to scroll while reading electronic texts, it is easy for them to accidentally skip passages. If students struggle with skipping passages, teach them to hold a finger or pencil up to the screen and track the text as they read it to stop their eyes from jumping. Note-taking and summarization can also be useful tools because they encourage students to pause and think about what they are reading and whether it makes sense, which will help them notice missing passages.

Digital texts often integrate extra resources into the material. For example, many texts allow students to see the definition of a word when they click on it; others offer links to illustrations, charts, and other resources that can help students understand complicated information. Teachers can encourage students to take advantage of these digital resources by demonstrating how to use them in class, reminding students to use them when they have questions during in-class readings, and asking guiding questions that require students to refer to them.

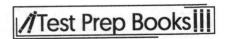

One of the central differences between print and electronic texts is that students can easily conduct keyword searches while reading online. To take advantage of this ability, students should learn to search for the information they need when rereading and skimming. Teachers can help students develop this skill by showing them how to generate keywords effectively. For example, searching for "brown beetles with pinchers" will be more effective than searching for simply "beetles."

Applying Reading Comprehension Skills for Varied Purposes

The first step toward comprehension is teaching students to apply a specific reading skill. However, comprehension strategies will prove worthless unless the students know how to apply them by themselves. Here are some strategies for helping students learn to apply reading comprehension skills.

Do not assume that students will simply know when and how to use a strategy. Instead, take time to explicitly teach them how to decide which reading strategies to use. For example, after teaching students about summarization and note-taking, ask them to think of contexts in which it would be helpful to use one of these skills. You could also provide your students with a reference chart detailing the different types of texts, how to recognize them, and useful strategies for reading them.

One of the best ways to train students to select appropriate strategies is to model your own thought process when you discuss texts as a class. Instead of saying, "Make sure to take notes on the six main points in this essay," you could say something like, "In the introduction, the author says he has six main points. Because the article is long, it would be easy to miss a main point or confuse it with a minor piece of evidence. So, to make sure we catch all six points, we'll take detailed notes as we read. Afterward, we can go through our notes and highlight the six major points." Once students have some experience with comprehension strategies, you can also have them model to each other by working collaboratively, asking them to suggest helpful strategies, and identifying what they want to learn from the text.

Regularly assess your students' comprehension to know which skills they need to develop, and then assign homework that will help them hone those skills. For example, an assessment might show that students struggle with literal comprehension. To address this problem, ask them to hand in their notes on a text. Teachers could then critique the notes, offering individualized suggestions to help students improve their reading skills.

Teachers can also use more informal assessments to find weaknesses in applying comprehension skills. For example, if only one student is able to answer an evaluative question asked during a class discussion, students are probably struggling with evaluative skills, such as analyzing the argument and recognizing point of view. In this case, teachers could review evaluative skills and then give students opportunities to practice using them in class. Alternatively, you might find that several students misinterpreted the literal meaning of a text in their homework because they did not know that "plastic" can mean "flexible" in older English. In this case, you could bring up the problem in class (keeping the students anonymous, of course) and remind your students that they can always look words up in a dictionary and check for alternative meanings when a text confuses them.

Reading Comprehension Skills and Strategies of Individual Students

Each child has their own particular learning needs, and therefore it is important for students to find strategies that work for them. One of the best ways to teach students to select the most effective comprehension strategies for themselves is to teach them metacognition. **Metacognition** is the process of thinking about one's own ideas, train of thought, or learning process. A student who thinks "I can

84

remember the events in a story easily, but I have trouble remembering the facts in science books" is displaying metacognition by thinking about their own learning process. Metacognition is an important skill for students because it enables them to identify their strengths and weaknesses and then select strategies that will help them learn effectively. For example, a student who realizes they are a visual learner can employ tactics such as visualization, drawing, and referring to charts and illustrations. On the other hand, a student who struggles to remember vocabulary could devote extra effort to making notes of new words and their definitions. You can teach metacognition by encouraging students to think about how they learn, modeling metacognition by describing your own thought processes, and inviting your students to experiment and find comprehension strategies that work for them.

Anticipating Student Needs

Although each student has different learning requirements, teachers can do their best to anticipate the needs of certain groups. Students often struggle with comprehension because of underlying learning disabilities, attention problems, or difficulties with reading. Teachers should try to identify and address these underlying issues, referring students to other professionals when appropriate.

When students are fluent readers but struggle with comprehension, teachers can help by building their general language skills. Teaching vocabulary can be particularly helpful because students sometimes struggle as the result of not understanding words. Teachers can also have students read out loud. Seeing and hearing the words at the same time allows students to absorb the information through two pathways, which boosts focus and comprehension. Finally, ask questions throughout the reading and have the students reread tricky passages. Questions during the reading help students stay on track. When you find that the student has missed something, you can go back and read it again together. This method helps the student learn to pay attention, self-question, and reread information when necessary.

English-language learners often need additional support with literal understanding of the text. For example, a student who does not know scientific words in English will have difficulty understanding a passage about chemistry, even if they have a good understanding of the subject. Complicated grammatical constructions can also pose a problem, particularly if the student's native language is markedly different from English. Teachers can help these students understand the text by teaching them vocabulary words in advance and helping them rephrase confusing constructions into simpler language. Teachers should also keep in mind that English-language learners, particularly older students, often have the background knowledge and critical-thinking skills they need to reach inferential and evaluative comprehension once they overcome the language barrier that makes literal comprehension difficult. Therefore, their comprehension often improves in rapid leaps as they learn new sets of words.

Gifted students who have above-grade reading skills often struggle with boredom. In this case, the problem is that the students *can* understand the material but *don't* because they find it too easy and are not motivated to understand it. To help these students stay motivated and engage with the material, teachers can encourage them to use additional resources or give the students additional **extension projects**. If the class is reading a book about lizards, for example, the teacher could give highly proficient readers a more challenging book on the subject and ask them to explore it after they have finished the assigned reading. Teachers can also help above-average students by giving them choices about their assignments. A teacher could give students the option to write either a summary or an evaluation of an article. This choice would allow students who have no difficulty understanding the article to stretch their skills by applying evaluative as well as literal comprehension skills.

Practice Quiz

1. Which of the following terms refers to techniques that allow students to progress toward a greater level of understanding on an increasingly independent level?
    a. Discourse
    b. Differentiation
    c. Scaffolding
    d. Benchmarking

2. Which of the following statements about literacy development is true?
    a. Research shows that literacy development begins as early as 3 months of age.
    b. Between 3 months and 6 months, babies begin to study a speaker's mouth and listen closely to speech sounds.
    c. Between 6 months and 9 months, babies can generally recognize a growing number of commonly repeated words, utter simple words, respond appropriately to simple requests, and begin to attempt to group sounds.
    d. Between 9 months and 12 months, babies rapidly strengthen their communication skills, connecting sounds to meanings and combining sounds to create coherent sentences.

3. Receptive language development refers to which of the following stages of literacy?
    a. Beginning literacy
    b. Early intermediate literacy
    c. Intermediate literacy
    d. Early advanced literacy

4. A reader is distracted from following a story because he is having trouble understanding why a character decided to cut school. He jumps to the next page to find out where the character is headed. This is an example of what?
    a. Directed reading-thinking activities
    b. KWL charts
    c. Metacognitive skills
    d. Self-monitoring comprehension

5. While studying vocabulary, a student notices that the words *circumference*, *circumnavigate*, and *circumstance* all begin with the prefix *circum–*. The student uses her knowledge of affixes to infer that all of these words share what related meaning?
    a. Around, surrounding
    b. Travel, transport
    c. Size, measurement
    d. Area, location

See answers on the next page.

Answer Explanations

1. C: *Scaffolding* refers to techniques that allow students to progress toward a greater level of understanding on an increasingly independent level by incrementally increasing difficulty and independence. *Discourse* is a general term that refers to oral or written communication, so Choice *A* is incorrect. *Differentiation* refers to tailoring instructional methods and activities toward individual students or different levels. Therefore, Choice *B* is incorrect. Choice *D* is incorrect because *benchmarking* refers to setting measurable standards during the learning process.

2. B: Choice *B* is a correct statement about the generally accepted progression of normal literacy development. Choice *A* is incorrect because research indicates that literacy development begins from birth, and that from birth to 3 months of age, babies start recognizing the sounds of familiar voices, and this actually begins the early stages of literacy development. Choices *C* and *D* are incorrect because those skills start developing a bit later than stated, between 9 months and 12 months of age for Choice *C*, and in the toddler years for Choice *D*.

3. A: Receptive language development is a term used to describe the beginning literacy stage, during which children begin understanding the "input" of language. This means that they start developing the ability to connect words with their meanings and comprehend spoken language that others say or read.

4. D: Scanning future portions of the text for information that helps resolve a question is an example of self-monitoring. Self-monitoring takes advantage of students' natural ability to recognize when they understand the reading and when they do not. Directed reading-thinking activities are done before and after reading to improve critical thinking and reading comprehension skills. KWL charts are used to help guide students to identify what they already know about a given topic. Metacognitive skills are when learners think about their thinking.

5. A: The affix *circum*– originates from Latin and means "around" or "surrounding. It is also related to other words that indicate something round, such as *circle* and *circus*.

Formal and Informal Methods for Assessing Reading Development

Data and Ongoing Reading Assessment

Instructors retrieve data from both informal and formal assessments. This data, whether written or gained through observation, is highly valuable in determining the effectiveness of teaching methods. Data-driven instruction guides reading improvement for all students simply because the data provides clear indications of where students are facing reading challenges or demonstrating strengths.

Differentiated instruction acknowledges that, while a group of students may be learning the same subject, the way each student learns and processes the subject is different. **Differentiation** involves looking at the different learning methods and reading areas and identifying which ones students respond to. Educators can then tailor, or differentiate, lessons to build on these skills and expedite the learning process. Differentiated instruction is divided into interest-based and ability-based instruction.

Much of a student's performance is based on their interest in the subject at hand. Sometimes a student may show difficulty reading because he or she isn't engaged in the material. One way to encourage reading growth is to allow students to choose their learning activities. This will give students ownership over their own education, enabling them to have fun and to use specific activities that help them improve their reading abilities. For example, students more interested in visual activities may find reading more beneficial than listening to oral reading exercises.

Ability-based differentiation focuses on three core areas that determine reading proficiency and build skill. The first area of focus examines students' conceptual understanding of reading. If a teacher uses vocabulary or reading comprehension exercises in class, they will be able to examine how students are performing and modify instruction to address any confusion. This can also indicate students' preferences as well. The second differentiation looks at how students analyze and use the reading. Instructors must look at how students respond to questions and whether their interpretation is accurate. The third differentiation looks at how students evaluate and perform reading, creating a reaction that responds to the reading. This differentiation looks particularly at interpretation with the added step of using this knowledge to write or say something that involves the reading without being prompted. Identifying issues in one of these areas will narrow down where more emphasis must be placed to improve reading skills. Each reading area will affect the other two; improving one differentiated area will impact the others.

Depending on what areas of difficulty the diagnostic data highlights, reteaching certain material is a promising starting point to help students overcome their reading issues. This isn't a step backward in instruction; it's an alteration. Differentiated instruction offers opportunities for students to relearn reading principles in ways that best fit them individually.

If students are having reading difficulties, the lessons can be modified to be clearer or address the specific areas of difficulty. Sometimes, this means teaching the material in a different way entirely. Recalling the areas of differentiated instruction, there are many components of reading skills and understanding. If a student is having difficulty in one area, such as reading analysis, building on

conceptual knowledge and performance/evaluation reading skills could help the student connect the gaps in analysis. For example, instead of just reading and responding to questions, students might grasp the material better through the use of simple logic. Breaking down sentence context and discussing the reading, rather than just asking questions and giving answers, can help bridge the gap in understanding, thus allowing students to draw further insight from the reading.

Considering what kind of activities improve which aspects of reading is also important. If students have phonetic problems, instructors should introduce activities that analyze the different aspects of words, as well as sounding out words, to build familiarity with English vocabulary and structure. To strengthen reading comprehension, incorporating activities that help students visualize what they read will help. Instructors should encourage students to paraphrase and summarize texts to examine their strengths and weaknesses as well. This will help the instructor identify what kind of differentiation may be necessary. Instead of shying away from challenging areas, it's important to modify lessons to help students approach the material with better focus and a renewed interest.

Student engagement will be instrumental in improving reading skills. Again, differential instruction encourages not only differentiated lessons and activities based on student ability, but also on interest. Having students design their own reading activities allows them to expand their skill sets while becoming eager to learn more. Activities such as synonym association for vocabulary words or even physically drawing out a given sentence will engage reading comprehension, analysis, and replication skills. Further assessments should be done to gauge the effectiveness of the new instruction methods.

Another way to differentiate instruction is through groups and collaboration when learning or reviewing reading material. In class, there are two forms of grouping instruction: teacher-based and student-based. A well-balanced and flexible learning environment will incorporate both types of grouping exercises to help students approach reading from multiple angles and practice problem-solving and critical-thinking skills. Students also strengthen social skills through flexible grouping.

Teacher-based grouping is organized by the instructor. This is the best method for introducing students to new material and exploring key concepts. Instructors may also choose to break the class up into small groups to provide instruction and work with students individually while the class is working. The goal here is to monitor students directly and provide differentiated instruction when necessary. This is the more variable of the two groupings and provides a more direct line for teacher intervention. However, students can also grasp concepts by interacting with their peers.

Student-based grouping focuses on students dictating the way the group is formed, essentially freeing the teacher to observe how they are interacting with others and approaching reading topics. This can be done by giving students the option to form their groups independently or by simply conducting a class discussion, which allows students to talk about the reading amongst themselves as opposed to merely listening to a lecture by the instructor. Posing questions for the class is a great way for students to learn correct answers and ask questions through simple conversation. Student-based groups are also excellent for school projects, allowing group members to pool their knowledge for success.

Flexible grouping relies on utilizing both teacher-based and student-based groupings throughout the instructional period. Using one more than the other isn't necessarily unbalanced, but the instructor should try to incorporate both groupings in order to broaden the students' experiences. The teacher's choice in using either method should also relate to how they are implementing differentiated teaching methods. Educators can combine the use of grouping to suit activities and lessons for all areas in which students may be facing difficulties in order to boost confidence and clarify material.

Criterion-Referenced and Norm-Referenced Tests

Teachers can assess their students' learning through both criterion-referenced and norm-referenced testing.

Criterion-Referenced Tests

Criterion-referenced tests compare children's performance to predetermined levels of competency. A reading test might compare first graders' skills to the guidelines for what students should know at the end of first grade. Criterion-referenced tests are a great way for teachers to measure student progress throughout the year. A teacher might administer the test during the first week of school and then again at the end of the first semester and at the end of the school year. The teacher could then compare the class's average scores as well as students' individual scores over those three tests to assess the class's progress.

One criterion-referenced assessment is the **Informal Reading Inventory (IRI)**. This test scores the student's ability to read and comprehend different texts. The test then uses the scores to determine four levels of reading: independent, instructional, frustration, and hearing capacity.

The **independent level** is the level of text the student can read without help and comprehend with 90 to 100% accuracy. This type of text is good for homework assignments. The **instructional level** is composed of texts the student reads but requires the teacher's help to read certain words. At this level, comprehension is at 70 to 85% accuracy. Because comprehension is nowhere near perfect, students should read texts at this level in class so the teacher can help them. At the **frustration level**, students struggle with reading, comprehension, or both. Comprehension is less than 70% accurate, and teachers should avoid this level of text. The **hearing comprehension level** measures the student's comprehension when they listen to texts that are read out loud. To avoid reaching the frustration level, students should be able to comprehend these texts with more than 70% accuracy.

Teachers use this test to determine students' abilities at the beginning of the year as well as to monitor their students' progress during the year. For example, a student might begin fourth grade with the ability to read *Amelia Bedelia* at the independent level and finish the year by reading *Charlotte's Web* at the same level. Because *Charlotte's Web* is significantly more complex than *Amelia Bedelia*, this change would show a marked improvement in the student's reading.

Norm-Referenced Assessments

Norm-referenced assessments compare individual students' scores to class, state, or national averages. These tests provide two types of information: how many questions the student answered correctly and a percentile rank.

Two of the most common norm-referenced tests are the SAT and the ACT. These tests analyze not only the percentage of questions students answered correctly but the percentile rank of each student. For example, the SAT has a score range of 400 to 1600. A student who scores 1000 answered approximately 88.7% of the questions correctly and ranks between the 40th and 50th percentile.

Validity, Reliability, and Bias in Testing

Several factors influence the accuracy of a test's results:

Validity is the accuracy with which a test represents students competencies. For instance, if a student who is a great reader takes a test and receives a poor score, the test probably has faults and was not valid.

Although there are many subtypes of validity, two are particularly important for teachers. **Construct validity** refers to a test assessing the skills it means to test. If a test claims to only measure reading skills but relies heavily on writing questions, it is not exhibiting construct validity. **Content validity**, on the other hand, means the test measures the full scope of the information it is assessing. For example, a teacher who has taught their students the consonants *b, c,* and *f* needs to test all three letters in order to create a test with content validity. If the test leaves out *f* or tests it far less than the other two letters, the test is not assessing an important element of the student's learning. To create truly valid tests, teachers need to ensure both construct and content validity, or, in other words, they need to test the right information and test across the scope of the information.

Reliability refers to whether a test's results are reproducible. Consider a student who takes different versions of the same test several times and has neither improved nor declined between testing sessions. If the student makes the same or similar scores, the test is reliable; it has yielded the same result through multiple trials. However, if the student makes markedly different scores, the test is not reliable.

Bias refers to factors that put certain students at a disadvantage. For example, a high school reading test that only measures students' ability to read scientific text will be far easier for students who excel in science than it will be for students who prefer humanities. To avoid this type of bias, teachers should use texts on a variety of subjects. Additionally, tests can be biased in ways that disadvantage minority students. For instance, a test based on reading samples that describe American holidays or food will disadvantage students whose families do not celebrate these events or eat those foods. When tests feature material that will be far more predictable to some students than others, they produce biased results.

Formal and Informal Reading-Related Assessments

Assessments are useful for identifying which students may be struggling with certain criteria as well as the specific areas of difficulty. Assessments can also indicate how well the material is being presented or provide vital clues on how to modify an individual student's instruction to help them grasp the content better. Generally, two types of assessments are used: informal and formal.

Informal assessments are not planned and lack a typical format or timeline. They can be as simple as watching and listening to how the students respond to answers in class or perform classwork. Observation is key. The instructor should perceive how students respond to reading and language concepts as well as how they interpret them. If a student isn't understanding something such as a cultural reading concept, it may indicate that a more in-depth explanation is required. This will help the teacher adapt the instruction to enable the student to self-correct their own performance.

Formal assessments are partially based on observation, but are planned and implemented with the design to see how students respond to specific stimuli. They give a clearer indication of students' strengths and weaknesses regarding the material. There are two primary methods for conducting formal

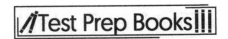

assessments. The most conventional is a simple pencil-and-paper test in which students read prewritten questions and respond to them in writing. These physical answers provide a direct window into what the students know and how their reading comprehension is progressing. **Performance assessments** are a little less concrete but can provide a lot of insight into the student's mind-set and reactions that are more three-dimensional than a written assessment. This method does not use written responses, but instead analyzes students' performance in response to reading questions or activities. When giving performance assessments, it's important to bear in mind key questions: Does the student understand what they just read? Did they seem uncomfortable when presenting their answer? How accurate was their response? From here, new teaching strategies can be implemented, or the instructor can identify ways to provide specialized assistance to boost students' skills.

Group Versus Individual Reading Assessments

Group testing refers to administering texts to multiple students at a time. A classic example of group testing would be a semester final in which everyone in the class takes the same test at the same time. Group testing is useful because it is time efficient and easy for teachers. The large volume of data these tests collect also allows teachers to create class averages and compare students' scores. Additionally, this kind of testing is typically more objective because it prevents the teacher from accidentally giving some students more help than others. However, there are some downsides to group testing. Because these tests almost always require students to read questions by themselves, they are weighted heavily on reading ability. This bias may pose a problem for younger students or those whose reading skills lag behind their other abilities. Group testing also prevents the teacher from connecting with individual students, which makes it hard for teachers to notice signs of learning disabilities. The lack of connection also prevents instructors from realizing that the student's results are atypical because a student is sleepy, sick, or simply having an off day. Overall, group testing is better for older students who already have good reading skills and is more suited for high-stakes assessments than screening and diagnostic testing.

Individual testing, on the other hand, requires the teacher to administer a test one-on-one. These tests usually involve the teacher, student, or both reading aloud. For instance, **assessments of phonemic awareness** are individual tests that measure a student's ability to recognize, isolate, and blend sounds. A phonemic awareness assessment includes questions such as "What is the first sound in the word 'bear'?" and "What word do these sounds make: /c/ /a/ /t/?" The first question measures **phoneme isolation** (the ability to realize that "b" is the first sound in "bear"), and the second assesses **blending** (putting the three sounds together into the word "cat"). Because these questions require the teacher to ask questions orally and listen to the student's response, they need to be conducted one-on-one. Individual testing is flexible and allows teachers to adjust the difficulty of the test so they can discover the student's exact level. These tests also allow the teacher to observe the student's behavior. A teacher might notice, for example, that the student's eyes are skipping ahead when they read, causing tracking problems and skipped words. However, this type of testing is time-consuming and more demanding for the teacher. Overall, individual testing is best when the teacher wants to gain detailed insight into a student's reading skills or process and is also an invaluable resource for testing young students who cannot yet read questions independently.

Assessing Particular Reading Skills

Letter-Sound Assessments

During **phoneme and letter-sound correspondence assessments**, teachers point to random letters or phonemes. The student is to then say the sound of the letter or phoneme and the teacher records the student's responses. Letter-sound combinations and phonemes with which a student, group, or class needs additional instruction and/or practice can be identified. The teacher can use this information to create lessons that emphasize the identified letter-sound correspondences and/or phonemes.

Phonics Assessments

Examples of ways to test a student's ability to decode words or readily read sight words include **Sylvia Green's Informal Word Analysis Inventory**, **Test of Word Reading Efficacy (TOWRE)**, and the **CORE Phonics Survey**. In these types of assessments, students are given a list of words and/or phonics patterns. Initially, high-frequency words that follow predictable phonics patterns are presented. Examples of **predictable phonics patterns** may include blending, word patterns, digraphs, etc. The words presented become more challenging as a student masters less difficult words. For example, a child may be assessed on their ability to decode nonsense words. The nonsense word assessments progress from decoding common sounds to less common sounds. Multisyllabic words within the assessments can reveal how well learners can chunk word parts through syllabication. As with other assessments discussed, the student's responses are recorded on a teacher's record sheet. In this way, the teacher can identify which word analysis principles and sight words a single student, a group of students, or an entire class is having difficulty with. These sight words, word parts, letter combinations, blending patterns, and/or syllabication principles can then be reinforced, retaught, reviewed, and practiced in future lessons. Additionally, the results of the assessment can be used to form instructional groups.

Informal Word Analysis Inventories

These can be used to assess encoding (spelling) of single-syllable words in the traditional manner. Students write the words that are read aloud by their teacher on a sheet of paper. In the early stages of spelling development, students are assessed on lists of words that are common to everyday language, share a word pattern or theme, and/or follow common orthographic patterns. The word lists become more complex as students demonstrate proficiency. The teacher can then plan instruction that targets the letter combinations and spelling patterns with which students are struggling. Such assessments can also be used to form instructional groups of students who share the same approximate developmental stage of spelling to better facilitate differentiated instruction.

As a general rule of thumb, isolated phonics tests should be given every four to six weeks. Spelling assessments can be given weekly or biweekly. Remediation should be implemented when students miss two or more questions on a five-question assessment and three or more questions on a ten-question assessment.

Contextualized Decoding Assessments

Despite the popularity of isolated decoding assessments, decoding should also be assessed in context. The **Word Recognition in Context** subtest of the Phonological Awareness Literacy Screening (PALS) is an example of an assessment that can be used for this purpose. During such assessments, passages that can be read by a student with 90% to 97% accuracy at acceptable rates are selected. The student reads these passages aloud to the teacher. By analyzing the student's approach to figuring out unknown words

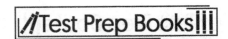

and the student's errors when reading a grade-appropriate passage, teachers are better able to determine which of the following three decoding strategies to emphasize during instruction:

- **Meaning cues** should be emphasized when a student fails to use context, story background, or pictures to assist in the decoding of new words.

- **Structural cues** are emphasized when a student does not use grammar or syntax to figure out an unknown word.

- **Visual cues** are emphasized when a student does not use grapheme or phoneme information to decode an unknown word. For example, a student may only read the beginning, middle, or end of words correctly (e.g., read *hat* as *cat*). A student may leave off a suffix or use incorrect yet similar letter combinations, indicating that visual cues need to be retaught.

Spelling Assessments

Similarly, spelling should be assessed within the context of a student's writing samples. When a student's spelling is assessed in the context of a writing assignment, a teacher is able to detect patterns of misconceptions and areas that need remediation. Such assessments can be used to detect the proper encoding of words as well as a student's vocabulary, diction, and syntax. By using a rubric, teachers are able to determine the student's developmental stage of spelling. Teachers can then create and implement spelling instruction that targets each student's individual strengths, weaknesses, and developmental stage of spelling.

Please note that once a student's areas of need are determined, any of the previously suggested phonics, sight word, and/or spelling strategies can be used for remediation and/or re-teaching of the identified skills.

Text Leveling

Text leveling means assigning levels to different texts. For example, a teacher might label books to denote their level and then arrange them on a bookshelf from simplest to most complex. This system would allow the teacher to always know the level of difficulty of the text they are assigning, and it would also help the teacher show students how to find books at the correct level during independent reading.

Leveling takes many factors into account. Although the next section will provide a more detailed analysis of these factors, they fall into three broad categories: qualitative factors, quantitative factors, and reader and task. **Qualitative factors** are subjective features of the text, such as whether the illustrations help guide readers toward comprehension and the level of background information required to understand the text. **Quantitative factors**, on the other hand, are objective facts about the text that can typically be expressed in numbers, such as the word count and average sentence length of the text. **Reader and reading task** refers to the connection between the student and the text. For example, a student who is passionate about chemistry will have an easier time reading a chemistry text than a student who hates the subject. Reader and task is a factor teachers must consider on a case-by-case basis because leveling systems cannot take students' interest and background knowledge into account. Therefore, teachers may sometimes need to mentally adjust the level of a text for individual students.

One common method of leveling is the **Learning A-Z Text Leveling System**, which rates books from aa (simple texts for kindergartners and raw beginners), through all the letters of the alphabet, to z^2 (complicated texts suitable for everyone from fifth graders to university students). Because the twenty-

nine levels of this system divide texts into such specific difficulty levels, teachers can use this method to closely measure small improvements within a grade level. Another leveling system is the **Lexile Text Measure**, which keeps a database of prose ranked from 200L (beginner) to 1200L (advanced). Lexile offers a test, the **Lexile Reading Measure**, that ranks students' abilities on the same scale so teachers can easily find appropriate books for them to read.

There are benefits and drawbacks to text leveling. On the positive side, leveling can motivate students. As they move up through the levels, they can see their own improvement and are motivated to keep reading. In a similar way, leveling enables teachers to easily recognize student progress and keep abreast of the levels of different students. Having a collection of books at different levels also allows teachers to quickly change reading materials if they find they are using text that is too difficult or too easy for a student. However, leveling can prevent students from reading books that interest them because those books may fall outside their level. Additionally, leveling can discourage struggling students who see that they are not improving.

Challenges and Supports in a Text

Illustrations help students piece together the meaning of a text. Pictures aid comprehension and can help students who struggle to form mental images. However, images can sometimes become a crutch. If students start guessing based on the picture rather than reading the text, teachers may need to begin only showing the picture after the students have read the section of text it depicts.

Predictable structures are common or repetitive elements in a text that allow students to guess what is about to happen. For example, many fairy tales contain a repeated statement, such as "Mirror, mirror on the wall," or feature similar events happening in a repetitive number: usually three or seven are popular numbers that have mythical or biblical connotations. Predictable structures make it easier for children to read and understand the text because they have a fairly good idea of what is going to come next.

Decodable text is text that has been designed to contain only sounds or words the students know. For example, decodable text might completely avoid the letter *j* because the students have not learned it yet. Naturally, this kind of text is easier for students. The downside is that the text can often be boring and repetitive, which leads to unengaged students.

Formatting is also important. If a text is broken into manageable paragraphs, it is easier for students to keep track of where they are in the reading. Students also gain a sense of accomplishment when they finish a section and can feel overwhelmed when they try to read a paragraph that is too long. Of course, the definition of "manageable sections" differs between ages and grade levels. Young and beginning readers need shorter sections, whereas older and more advanced readers can handle longer chunks of text.

The **content** of a text influences its difficulty. If the piece features events or themes that are too complex for young children to grasp, it is too difficult for them, even if the text itself is simple.

There are also many quantitative factors that make texts more or less challenging. The average number of words in a sentence can be a good way to judge text complexity. If the average sentence has few words, the text features simple constructions that will not overwhelm beginning readers. A longer average sentence length, however, indicates that the text contains complicated sentences that may be too difficult for beginners.

The total word count of a text also provides information about its complexity. With some exceptions, longer texts are more difficult. If nothing else, beginning readers will become tired and overwhelmed while reading a long book.

Some books also contain supports that help students comprehend them. A built-in glossary, for example, aids student understanding by explaining difficult words. Other supports include chapter summaries and reviews, key terms that are bolded so students know they are important, and charts and graphs that help students visualize the material.

Determining Independent, Instructional, and Frustration Reading Levels

As previously described, the IRI assesses children's reading to determine four different comprehension levels: independent, instructional, frustration, and hearing.

To determine a student's levels, teachers need to administer an IRI. To prepare for the test, select an IRI or make your own. Make sure the texts start at a level that is too easy for the student (one or two grade levels below their level), and then continue to levels you know will be too difficult. The texts should also be on a variety of subjects to avoid bias based on background knowledge or culture. If you are making your own IRI, count the number of words in the texts and write enough high-quality comprehension questions to accurately assess the student's understanding.

While the student is reading, keep track of how many words they read incorrectly. You do not need to record which words the student got wrong, just how many were missed. Try not to make a fuss over every mistake, because this may distract the student or affect their confidence. Tick marks are a great way to record this information quietly. Once the student has completed reading each section, ask the comprehension questions and document whether the answers are correct.

When the student is making frequent errors (i.e., reading 10% of words incorrectly) and obviously struggling, you can help them finish the section and then stop the test. The student is clearly at the frustration level, and reading further will be pointless and discourage the student.

You can calculate reading accuracy scores in the following way:

$$(Total\ number\ of\ words - number\ of\ words\ missed) \div (total\ number\ of\ words\,) \times 100$$

You can score the comprehension questions as you would score any other test. The result should be a percentage.

After you have conducted and scored the test, you can compare the student's scores to the benchmarks for each level. At the independent level, students comprehend the text with at least 90% accuracy. They can also read the text aloud with an accuracy of 95% or more. At the instructional level, comprehension is at 70 to 85% accuracy and reading is 90 to 94%. At the frustration level, comprehension is less than 70% and reading is less than 90% accurate.

Approaches to Reading Instruction

Theories, Approaches, Practices, and Programs for Reading Skills and Comprehension

Jean Piaget's Stages of Cognitive Development

Jean Piaget's stages of cognitive development map the stages through which children move as they mature. Teachers can use this theory to see what information their students are capable of understanding.

In the **sensorimotor stage** (birth to 2 years), children understand the world through their senses. For example, a baby gains information about an object not by thinking about its material and use but by putting the object in their mouth. The major insight children gain during this stage is **object permanence**, which is the realization that things still exist, even when they are not visible. A baby who does not understand object permanence will probably cry when a toy slides under the couch because they believe it has been lost forever. A child with object permanence, however, will realize the toy still exists, even though they cannot see it.

In the **preoperational stage** (2–7 years), children begin to think symbolically. **Symbolic thought** is the capacity to realize that one thing stands for another. For instance, children might display symbolic thought by pretending that a box is a ship. Preoperational children gain language skills, but they are **egocentric**, struggling to empathize with others.

In the **concrete operational stage** (7–11 years), children finally begin to think logically. They can understand **conservation**, which is the idea that the same amount of a substance can look different in different forms. For example, a child who understands that the same amount of water looks different in a tall skinny vase and a squat vase understands conservation.

In the **formal operational stage** (11 to adulthood), children see the development of theoretical thought. They can think about ideas such as "freedom" or "evil," form logical arguments, and consider hypothetical, or "what if," situations.

Schema Theory

Another important theory is **schema theory**, which is a way of understanding the acquisition of knowledge. This theory is particularly applicable to reading comprehension. A **schema** is a network of information a child uses to understand the world. For example, the descriptive facts "has four legs" and "for one person to sit in" are part of the schema that allows a child to recognize that an object is a chair. Schema theory posits that, when children learn, they are integrating new knowledge into their existing schemata. For instance, a child encountering a rolling office chair for the first time could integrate "may be on wheels" into their chair schema. When applied to reading comprehension, this theory emphasizes students' background knowledge. If a student is having trouble with comprehension, he or she probably has incomplete or incorrect schema. For example, a child who has never seen a daffodil might be unable to understand a poem about the flower simply because they have no schema to refer back to for background information. Alternatively, a child might not understand a passage because they have a faulty schema that does not draw a distinction between sheep and goats. Reading materials at the correct level will help children expand and refine their schemata; however, teachers need to be mindful of individual students and address gaps in their background knowledge that will prevent them from misunderstanding the text.

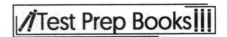

Situational Learning Theory

There are also theories about the ideal learning context for student success. **Situational Learning Theory** suggests that students learn information best and are most able to apply it when they learn that information in a context similar to the actual environment in which they will apply their knowledge. This theory argues that students have difficulty retaining abstract knowledge; instead, they thrive on information that helps them navigate practical scenarios. Situational Learning Theory also emphasizes communal learning because students can act out realistic scenarios together and receive feedback and help from others (e.g., through role-playing or group work). Teachers can apply this theory by creating a learning context that replicates real-life scenarios. A math teacher could teach their students to perform addition by having them play store and calculate totals and change. Similarly, a teacher could have students study the vocabulary words they are learning in context. For instance, students could practice new words related to plants by collaboratively making a flyer describing the plants in the school grounds.

Engagement Theory

A related concept is **Engagement Theory**. This theory posits that students are most engaged when they are completing worthwhile tasks in a collaborative way. Any project should have three traits. It should be collaborative, project-based, and authentic, as described below:

- **Collaborative**: Students should work in a group so they can learn social skills and help each other.

- **Project-Based**: The work involves using a variety of skills to address an issue, such as researching and then writing a paper.

- **Authentic**: The project should be interesting and meaningful to people other than the students.

Take the example of students making a flyer about plants. This project meets the three criteria of engagement theory because the students are working together (collaborative); using a variety of skills, such as research, writing, and spelling (project-based); and creating work that is applicable to the real world and interesting to other people (authentic).

Connectivism

Connectivism is a theory about how students relate to technology. Connectivism argues that the internet is like a huge social network. Students can contribute knowledge to the collective understanding, like by answering questions on forums, and they can also gain knowledge, like by finding the answers to their own questions. This theory suggests that teachers can use technology, such as online forums and collaborative note-taking, to help students form peer networks in which they support each other's learning. For example, a teacher could implement connectivism by asking students to post a question and answer somebody else's question every week in a class forum.

Approaches to Teaching Reading

There are three common approaches to teaching children how to read:

The **bottom-up approach** argues that children read by decoding, or recognizing the individual sounds letters make and then blending them together. This method of teaching the sounds of letters is called phonics.

98

The **top-down approach** (or **whole-language theory**) suggests that reading is educated guessing. This approach teaches students to recognize sight words, or short, common words, such as "can" or "still."

The **integrated approach** combines the bottom-up and top-down approaches. Students may learn some sight words, but they also learn phonics so they can sound out new words by themselves. The integrated approach is currently the most popular approach to reading instruction.

Reading programs are curricula designed to teach children how to read. They typically follow the three approaches outlined above and also include **intervention programs**, which are designed to help struggling students or prevent at-risk students from falling behind, as well as programs for gifted students who find the classroom material too easy.

Here are a few practices that can help students build strong reading and comprehension skills:

Reading out loud is helpful, both when the teacher is reading to the class and students are reading aloud. When students listen without having to read, they are able to focus on comprehension and build vocabulary they would not encounter in texts easy enough for them to read. Having students read aloud is also useful because hearing and seeing the words at the same time builds neural connections and makes it easier for them to focus.

Multisensory instruction is like reading out loud in that it helps children absorb information through multiple pathways. Multisensory instruction helps children learn by involving as many senses as possible. For example, a teacher might say the sound /r/, write the letter *r* on the board, and then have children form the letter out of play dough or walk in its shape before writing it on paper. Although multisensory instruction is particularly useful for students who have learning disabilities or are struggling, it can help all students.

Assessing the Reading Development of Individual Students

Student performance from entry-level assessments should be used to identify if students have already mastered a skill before instruction on that skill begins. If all students perform well on questions that pertain to a particular standard or benchmark, then less focus can be given to that standard or benchmark. In this way, more instructional time can be allotted for standards and benchmarks on which students have yet to show mastery.

Observations should be made regularly during progress monitoring and guided practice. Such observations can be recorded in a grade book and referenced in order to determine student gaps in understanding to guide future instruction. During guided practice, the teacher should also provide students with explicit feedback. Students should apply the teacher's recommendations as those recommendations are made. Such feedback gives students a chance to begin to assess their own understanding of the skill; then, the skill is tested through a summative assessment.

Each question on a summative assessment should be linked to a particular standard or benchmark. Student responses per question on standard-aligned summative assessments should be charted and analyzed. In this way, teachers can determine which standards or benchmarks have not yet been mastered by an entire class, a group of students, or an individual. If an entire class responded incorrectly to a question that is in alignment with an identified standard, then that concept needs to be retaught to the entire class. Teachers can also use data gathered from standard-aligned summative assessments to identify which students require remediation or can be advanced within the course of study.

Data from all forms of assessment should be used to form leveled groups. The groups should be dynamic. Thus, as student performance changes, the grouping of students should also change. In this way, all students can be ensured to receive proper intervention of the particular standard(s) or benchmark(s) with which they struggle. This, in turn, increases opportunities for students to master each skillset.

Differentiating Reading Instruction

Students with Reading Difficulties

Small group intervention is necessary for students who are struggling with reading comprehension. Struggling students need to meet with the teacher more frequently and for longer periods of time to remediate skills that have yet to be mastered. Teacher "read alouds" provide students time to listen to the storyline, characters, setting, plots, sequence of events, and conclusions, without having to decode the words themselves, which aids comprehension. Teachers should also play games or complete review worksheets with students in a one-to-one setting because it provides additional time to secure skills and gives students privacy to ask questions regarding the lesson.

Students with Special Needs

Students with special needs may need individual differentiated instruction settings to cater to specific needs. Effective teachers create and use assignments based on their students' needs. First, teachers must identify the skill(s) that need extra assistance. Then, instructors should use short texts at each student's level that can be read aloud and discussed. For special needs students, key elements of a story should be broken down into categories such as characters, setting, plot, conflict, and resolution. With teacher support, students can use story maps to fill in information on their own. As students fill in important details, the teacher can stop to address each before continuing to read, which will allow students to recreate images as the teacher reads. Students at lower levels should support their answers through group discussions; that way, their frustration levels will not peak.

English Learners and Speakers of Nonstandard English

English Language Learners should identify words and vocabulary before they can comprehend. Pre-teaching vocabulary prior to reading a given text can help students understand the overall text better. Figurative language and inferential skills are especially difficult, as they can be culturally dependent. Teaching the underlying meanings of the text is often the most challenging task, as clarifying cultural content is necessary.

Needs of Advanced Learners

Advanced learners should be challenged. One way to challenge advanced learners is to provide texts that may include challenging vocabulary or obscure ideas that require students to rely on inference and prediction skills in order to read between the lines. Another way for teachers to challenge advanced leaners is to expand assignments by adding more questions, skills, and strategies that require a higher level of thought. Activities that promote inferential and figurative analysis skills can create great discussion between peers and encourage higher-level thinking skills.

Reading Instruction Based on Ongoing Assessment

Ongoing assessment means testing students throughout the year and using the results to improve lesson plans. For instance, a teacher who finds that 90% of the class missed a question about fractions can be fairly sure that the lesson on that topic was not clear enough. The teacher can then take two

steps: reviewing the misunderstood material with the class and improving the lesson so next year's class will not face the same issue.

The first step to both of these steps is reflection. Teachers should analyze where their students went wrong to find out where the gap in their knowledge lies. For instance, if students are able to define a word correctly but spell it wrong, it is likely that the teacher did not spend enough time on spelling. Sometimes the problem will not be so obvious, and teachers will need to spend more time looking back on their lesson plans and trying to find aspects that might have confused students. For example, a teacher might find that they missed an important point, moved over material too quickly, or explained a topic in language that was too complicated for students to understand.

Once teachers have found the weaknesses in their lesson, they are ready to move on to reteaching or reviewing the material. If a significant number of the students have not grasped the material, reteaching is necessary. Teachers should approach the material as if it were entirely new. If the students seem to have a general understanding of a topic but are foggy about the details, teachers can simply review by highlighting key points of the information.

To make this kind of adjustments easier, teachers should build flexibility into their syllabus. Adjustments are inevitable, and teachers can avoid difficult rescheduling by allowing time for review and not setting their plans in stone.

Instructional Strategies for Particular Reading Skills

Often, students struggle with some areas of reading more than others. By isolating these areas of difficulty and helping students improve them, teachers can improve their students' reading competency quickly. Here are some individual skills and ways to target them:

Phonological awareness is the ability to recognize sounds and syllables. A child who can tell that the /a/ sound in "cat" is the same as the /a/ sound in "cast" or understand how many syllables are in a word is demonstrating phonological awareness. Children with phonological awareness can also blend sounds together to form words. For example, if the teacher says /s/, /u/, /n/, the child can recognize the word "sun". Children who struggle to blend words while reading are usually struggling with phonological awareness.

Similarly, **phonemic awareness** is the ability to manipulate individual sounds. For example, a student who recognizes that you can make the word "as" into "ask" by adding the sound /k/ is demonstrating phonemic awareness. Both phonological and phonemic awareness are oral skills children need to read effectively. If they are unable to recognize and manipulate sounds, they will be unable to read fluently. Games are a good way to teach both types of awareness. You could work on phonological awareness, for example, by clapping syllables, which is saying words slowly while clapping at each syllable, such as saying "po-ta-to" with three claps. For students who can read individual letters but struggle to piece those sounds into words, blending exercises are useful. Practice saying individual sounds and having the student form them into a word. Games are also useful for phonemic awareness. For instance, you could spell out a word with letter tiles and then ask the student to form a new word by moving a tile.

Phonics skills are also an important component of reading. Students need to know the sounds of letters before they can sound out words. If a student cannot recognize individual letters or **phonograms**, flash cards and reading drills in which the student reads multiple words that feature the same sound can be helpful. Often, students struggle with letters that can make multiple sounds, such as *a, c,* or *j*. Teachers

101

can help students learn these sounds by listing the sounds a letter can make and comparing them, like the /a/ sounds in "cat," "case," and "call." **Chunking** is a way of visually separating the syllables in a word. Chunking is useful because it helps students practice vowel sounds. For example, the word "salutation" chunks into "sal-u-ta-tion." Chunking this word helps students understand that the letter *a* makes a long sound when it is at the end of a syllable in "ta" but a short sound when it is in the middle of the syllable "sal."

Word identification means the ability to read words automatically, or with minimal effort. Instead of consciously sounding out every letter and then blending them together, students with word identification use phonetic processes on a subconscious level. The key to word identification is repetition. Students need to read words many times before they can read them automatically, so rereading books is a great way to build this skill. Teachers can also select books that use the same vocabulary words or have students read and reread word lists.

Vocabulary knowledge allows students to read words more easily and understand what they are reading. One way to build students' vocabulary is to read aloud to them because this activity allows them to encounter words that are beyond their reading level. Reading materials on a variety of topics is also important because it exposes students to the specialized vocabulary in many areas.

Automatic Recognition of High-Frequency Sight Words

Unlike word identification, the **automatic recognition of sight words** is not a phonetic process. Rather than sounding out a word subconsciously, students do not sound the word out at all. Instead, they recognize the word by its familiarity and context. But like word identification, this skill depends on repetition and improves when children reread texts. Flash cards and pictures paired with images can also be useful.

Beginning readers enter primary school years with many challenges involving literacy development. Tackling the alphabetic principle and phonemic awareness helps children to recognize that specific sounds are usually comprised of specific letters, or a combination thereof, and that each letter or combination of letters carries a specific sound. However, these young readers are also faced with the challenge of sight word mastery. **Sight words** do not necessarily follow the alphabetic principle and appear quite often in primary reading material. Some sight words are decodable, but many are not, which requires the additional challenge of memorizing correct spelling. Some of these non-decodable sight words include words such as *who, the, he, does,* and so on. There are approximately one hundred sight words that appear throughout primary texts.

The goal for primary teachers is to help emergent readers to recognize these sight words automatically, in order to help strengthen reading fluency. One effective instructional approach is to provide children daily opportunities to practice sight words in meaningful contexts and to establish a clearly visible, large print word wall that children can freely access throughout the day. Dr. Edward William Dolch was a well-known and respected children's author and professor who, in the late 1940s, published a list of sight words he believed appeared most frequently in children's literature for grades kindergarten through second grade. Now known as the Dolch Word List, these sight words are still widely used in primary classrooms throughout the United States. Organized by grade and frequency, the Dolch Word List consists of 220 words in total, with the first one hundred known as the "Dolch 100 List." Dr. Edward Fry, a university professor, author, and expert in the field of reading, published another commonly used high-frequency word list approximately a decade later. Although similar in many ways to the Dolch List, the Fry Word List primarily focuses on sight words that appear most frequently in reading material for third to ninth grade. Other high-frequency word lists now exist, but the Dolch and Fry word lists are still

widely used in today's elementary classrooms. The debate, however, is whether to teach high-frequency sight words in isolation or as part of the integrated phonics program.

Unlike many sight words, **decodable words** follow the rules of phonics and are spelled phonetically. They are spelled precisely the way they sound—as in words like *dad* and *sit*. When a child has mastered their phonics skills, these decodable words can also be easily mastered with continued opportunities to practice reading. Activities involving segmenting and blending decodable words also help to strengthen a child's decoding skills. Some educators will find that it is beneficial to integrate lessons involving decodable words and high-frequency sight words, while others may see a need to keep these lessons separate until children have demonstrated mastery or near mastery of phonemic awareness. Some activities that encourage the memorization of sight words and strengthen decoding skills involve the use of flash cards, phonemic awareness games, air writing, and card games, such as *Bingo* and *Go Fish*.

Both the Dolch and Fry word lists are organized according to frequency and grade level. It is widely accepted that educators should follow a cumulative approach to reading instruction, introducing high-frequency sight words that are also phonetically decodable. Should words appear in the lesson that are not phonetically decodable, educators may wish to use this as an opportunity to evaluate the children's phonemic awareness skills and determine whether or not students are ready for lessons that integrate non-decodable sight words. For instance, an educator might challenge a student to study the parts of the non-decodable sight word by asking whether or not there are parts of the word that are phonetically decodable and parts that are not. This approach gives students the opportunity for guided word study and acts as a bridge between phonemic awareness skills and sight word memorization.

Determining what lists of words to introduce to students varies greatly and depends on an initial and ongoing spelling assessment of each child to determine their current spelling and reading levels. Effective instructional approaches also involve the intentional selection of words that demonstrate a specific spelling pattern, followed by multiple opportunities to read, spell, segment, and blend these word families. Students will benefit the greatest with ongoing formative and summative assessments of their decoding skills as well as their ability to apply their word knowledge to and memorize non-decodable sight words. **Formative assessment** monitors student understanding during a period of instruction; it is generally fairly informal. **Summative assessment** tests student understanding against a generally accepted standard or benchmark at the end of an instructional segment and is often more formal than formative assessment.

With the reinforcement of high-frequency word walls, daily opportunities to read, write, and engage in meaningful word games and activities, children will gradually begin to develop their reading and spelling skills and learn to become more fluent and capable readers.

When students are invited to become word detectives, the study of root words and affixes is of prime importance. There are several instructional approaches to the study of root words and affixes, including a multi-sensory guided approach in which children can physically pull apart the affixes to be left with the root word and then manipulate the root word by playing with a variety of suffixes and prefixes. The following table begins with the original word containing both a prefix and suffix. The word is pulled

apart into its individual components—root, prefix, and suffix. Then, it is given a new prefix and suffix to form a new word, carrying a completely new meaning:

Original Word	Root Word	Prefix	Suffix	New Prefix	New Suffix	New Word
inactive	act	in	ive	De	ate	deactivate
disbelieving	believe	dis	ing	Un	able	unbelievable
unbearable	bear	un	able	For	ing	forbearing

Effective instruction for root, prefix, and suffix study should involve the active exploration of words, with ample opportunity for children to read the words in meaningful context. Typically, a formal study of root words and affixes is introduced by the 4th grade, but it may be introduced earlier, depending on the students' understanding of basic phonics and spelling patterns. It is important for educators to keep in mind that new vocabulary terms, verb forms, plurals, and compound words may present a challenge for some students.

A formal study of root words, prefixes, and suffixes strengthens a child's knowledge of word meanings, expands vocabulary knowledge, and advances their understanding and application of various spelling patterns. Children will learn more about how affixes affect the spelling of the root word and can completely alter its meaning, which ultimately strengthens their ability to read, write, and spell accurately and effectively. As children become familiar with various affixes, they will begin to decipher the meaning of unfamiliar words that share the same affixes and roots.

Close Reading and Rereading

Of course, reading is more than the ability to accurately sound out words. Unless students are able to understand or analyze the texts they read, they will not benefit from their reading. Additionally, students who do not fully grasp their reading material will be less interested in reading because they are missing the most exciting aspect. Because students of different ages have different abilities, **close reading** will look different at different ages. For example, first graders will probably evaluate material by comparing it to their own experiences, whereas sixth graders will have the background knowledge and abstract thinking skills to analyze the author's argument and the validity of the author's evidence.

Rereading can also be a great way to develop students' reading skills. As previously mentioned, rereading also helps build word recognition by exposing children to the same words several times. Therefore, it is a great way to improve your students' reading fluency. Rereading can also improve student engagement. Children thrive on repetition. They often play the same game again and again, perform repetitive play activities, or rewatch the same movie. Rereading is a great way to appeal to children's love for repetition, and often students will enjoy a book more when they read it repeatedly. In addition, rereading aids comprehension by allowing students to understand pieces of information that eluded them during the first reading. For example, a student might not know what "verdant" meant the first time they read a text and only learn the word by asking a question after finishing the book. Rereading the text would allow the student to fully understand the author's meaning.

Finally, close reading and rereading teach students the skills they need to become good writers. By studying how authors build arguments, characters, or setting, students learn how to create compelling

work. In a similar way, rereading familiarizes children with the vocabulary and construction of high-quality texts. This mental library of good writing will serve as a reference guide when students begin to write themselves. You cannot expect students to produce good work if they have not consumed great texts that they can learn from and emulate.

Because close reading and rereading demand plenty of effort and time from students and shape their future writing, it is important for teachers to pick texts that are genuinely worthwhile. Nobody wants to reread a boring or poorly written text, and focusing on material that contains mistakes or is poorly written will influence students' writing for the worse.

Evaluating and Sequencing Texts for Reading Instruction

Often, teachers who want to find the level of a text can refer to the databases of widely respected leveling systems, such as the Lexile Text Measure or the Learning A-Z Text Leveling System. However, sometimes teachers want to read a new book that does not yet appear on these databases or find that their classes have special requirements that make the usual text leveling systems inadequate. Sometimes, teachers only need a general idea of how difficult a text is, not a systematic breakdown of every aspect. In these cases, it can be better for teachers to conduct their own evaluations of text complexity. To accurately evaluate and sequence texts, teachers need to account for both qualitative and quantitative factors.

Qualitative Factors

A central qualitive factor is **level of meaning**. This term refers to how much analytical thought a text demands of its reader. A young children's book about farm animals probably does not require its readers to look for figurative meanings or evaluate arguments; instead, it simply presents enjoyable facts or events, and students only need literal comprehension to grasp its meaning. However, more complex literature requires inferential and evaluative skills. For example, even if children are able to read and understand the literal meaning of *Gulliver's Travels*, they will miss the main point of the book unless they are also able to understand allegory and satire.

Vocabulary is also an important factor in text complexity. Reading is a great way for students to learn new words, but texts with too many unfamiliar vocabulary words can be overwhelming. Conversely, a book with no challenging vocabulary is likely too easy.

Text structure also affects how difficult a text is. For example, although a book that often switches narrators or has flashbacks may be too confusing for younger students, these same complexities in the structure would be entertaining to an older class.

Quantitative Factors

Teachers often determine a text's difficulty by using **readability formulas**, which are mathematical equations designed to calculate the complexity of a text's language objectively. One popular readability formula is the **Fry Readability Formula**, which measures the length of sentences in words. To use this formula, teachers select three random passages of one hundred words each. They then count the number of sentences and syllables in each passage and calculate the average numbers of sentences and syllables per one hundred words. Finally, they chart the resulting two numbers on a **Fry Graph**, which

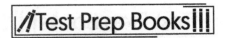

turns the data into a numeric score that estimates the grade level for which the text would be suitable, as in the example below.

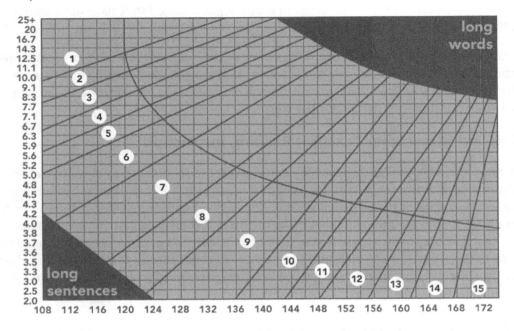

Another good readability formula is the **Flesch-Kincaid Grade Level**, which also examines sentence and word length.

$$Flesch - Kincaid\ Grade\ Level = (0.39 \times average\ sentence\ length) + (11.8 \times average\ word\ length) - 15.59$$

Scores below 12.9 are equivalent to grade levels (find the grade level by rounding down). Texts from 12.0 to 15.9 are typical of texts students read in college, and 16.0 to 17.9 reflect the reading abilities of college graduates. Texts above 18.0 are written at a professional level.

When using any readability formula, make sure you are balancing the results with a qualitative analysis. These formulas only measure text complexity, and many challenging books are written in simple language.

Once you have determined the levels of the texts you want to use, you can begin **sequencing**, or deciding the order in which your students should read the texts. In general, you should sequence in order of easiest to hardest text so your students will read more difficult material as their reading skills improve. However, there is room for flexibility. As long as no text is at the frustration level, you can switch books around a little if the order would make more sense because of a historical timeline, holiday or seasonal themes, etc.

Balancing Exposure Between Literary and Informational Texts

Cultivating a healthy balance between literary and informational texts is important for the well-being of both the class as a whole and individual students. Your class includes all kinds of students. Some are talented in science, others in the humanities, and some in both areas. These students will need different skills when they pursue further education or a career, and the best way you can fill all these different requirements is by cycling between different types of text. For example, a student who is going to

106

become a statistician would find strategies for reading informational texts particularly helpful for building skills that will be necessary in their career. In a similar way, a student who is going to be an actor would derive special benefit from analyzing literary texts, and a future historian would need to know how to analyze both informational and literary texts. By exposing your students to different types of texts and teaching them the skills they need to analyze these works, you are preparing them for their university studies and careers.

Although different students will find different types of reading preparational for their future careers, all students benefit from a balanced mixture of literary and informational reading. Even if a student is going to become an artist and never touch an informational text ever again, they will be interacting with facts by reading the news and talking to other people. Unless the student knows how to analyze facts and interpret data, they will not be prepared to form well-thought-out views on current issues, hold intelligent conversations, or create logical arguments. In a similar way, a student who goes into chemistry and hates literature will still benefit from the close-reading skills and ability to interpret characters that literature teaches. Essentially, informational and literary texts teach slightly different kinds of critical-thinking skills, and a well-rounded person needs both types to succeed in the world. Finally, most people do not fall at extreme ends of the spectrum. If someone specializes in informational work, they can enjoy reading literature, and vice versa. Even if students are not using the skills you taught them in their future careers, these abilities may give them hobbies and passions that enrich their lives.

Large-Group, Small-Group, and Individualized Reading Instruction

Large-group reading instruction is great for teaching visual concepts for the first time. For example, you can explain that the letter *a* makes the sound /a/ to a large group of students effectively. However, large groups are not ideal for teaching activities that involve listening to students or conducing remedial instruction. For instance, if you are running a phonemic awareness activity that involves saying sounds and having students blend them into words, a large group will prevent you from working with every student. Additionally, large groups can make it difficult for shy students to participate in class. That being said, large-group work is efficient and allows teachers to ensure that students are all learning the same thing. Overall, it is best to use large-group instruction in situations in which you do not need to provide personalized instruction or feedback.

Conversely, **small-group work** (usually groups of four to six students) is ideal for personalized lessons and feedback. Although teachers cannot cater to the needs of each student during large-group lessons, small-group work allows them to break students into groups based on ability or other needs and then teach to a group of similar children. For example, you might help struggling students by giving them an introduction to the topic before you teach it to the whole group. This lesson would allow the students to learn the information more effectively and feel competent. You can also use small-group work to review by grouping your students by their weakest area on an assessment and then reteaching or reviewing with each group. Small-group work is also a great idea in situations in which you need to provide feedback, especially if you have a large class. For example, you could provide more detailed feedback to more students by asking them to summarize a story in small groups and then talking with each group individually.

Finally, **individual reading instruction** is particularly helpful when teachers need to hear sounds or provide individualized instruction. When teaching reading to a large class, it can sometimes be difficult to hear every student and make sure they are all making the correct sounds. For example, a student could be confusing the sounds /g/ and /j/ in a large group, and the teacher might not notice this

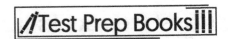

mistake. Individual instruction is good for checking in on your students and making sure you have not missed this type of hidden mistake. Individual instruction is also ideal for exceptional students, students with challenges such as learning disabilities who may feel lost in large groups, and accelerated learners who become bored. By teaching individual students, you can provide remedial and accelerated lessons that are tailored to suit the needs of each student.

Selecting Meaningful Reading Materials

When possible, it is best to let students have at least some say in the books you will read as a class. For example, you could pick three suitable books and then have students vote on which one they wanted to read. Giving students a choice in their assignments ensures that the texts are appealing to them and allows them to choose texts that align with their interests. These benefits boost engagement and make students more likely to start reading independently at home.

Additionally, it is helpful to consider where students are coming from and try to understand their background and interests. For example, if the majority of your students live in rural areas and are growing up on farms, their interests and background knowledge will be different from those of children who grew up in a major city. If you are reading a book about cows, children who have grown up with cows will need much less supplemental information and support than children who have never seen one. But although introducing children to subjects that are outside the scope of their daily lives can be challenging and take more time, students are often equally (or even more) engaged while reading about a new and exciting topic. Therefore, you need to take your students' interests into account as well as their background. Just because you are living in the inland United States does not mean that the students have no interest in ocean life or do not want to learn about other countries.

It is also important to include multicultural literature in your classroom. Multicultural literature is literature that teaches students to learn about and accept people from various backgrounds. For example, multicultural literature includes characters from different cultures and minority ethnic groups. Including multicultural literature has two benefits. It helps students from minority groups feel included and seen, and it fosters cultural awareness and respect in all of your students. The books you choose for class can certainly reflect the diversity in your classroom and city, but they can also engage with cultures that students might encounter elsewhere in the United States and abroad. Introducing children to people and cultures who are different from them is beneficial because it broadens their minds, and therefore you do not need to worry about only choosing cultures with which your students will have personal interactions.

Promoting Reading Development Through Environment

Creating a Literacy-Rich Environment
Projects and presentations are great ways to create a literacy-rich environment where reading is promoted. Projects and presentations should also meet the speaking and writing components of the framework for ELA in the state where the reading instructor works. Additionally, projects and presentations encourage students to use reading and research as an avenue through which they can set and pursue personal goals.

Presentations can include digital and technology components, such as PowerPoint®, Glogster, Powtoon, or recorded videos. Projects may be presented as a "grab bag" or tic-tac-toe board that include several options that students can choose to complete. In this way, students can pick projects that meet their

individual abilities, goals, and interests. Allowing students to choose from a set group of options also promotes differentiation within a class.

Rather than utilizing reading groups, students can be arranged into book clubs, author studies, literature circles, or other discussion groups. All members of such groups can read the same text together or independently. Either way, the group's members or entire class should come together at some point each week to discuss the selected text.

Support Systems Available to Promote Skillful Teaching of Reading

Professional development (PD) opportunities are often used to expose teachers to strategies that can be used to promote skillful teaching of reading. Sometimes administrators offer incentives for teachers to attend after-school PD courses. Such incentives may include extra pay, credits to advance degrees or salary, or free materials and resources. If money is a factor, schools may be able to receive tuition compensation when teachers take courses that are specific to the schools' goals. Either way, PDs enable teachers to collaborate with coworkers or teachers from other grade levels or schools in order to learn from one another.

Grade-level teams and meetings are other ways that teachers can sit down with peers to share materials, ideas, and resources. If students within a grade level are struggling with a particular standard, it is more economical and efficient to address this concern across a grade level. Grade-level teams may be able to order materials with provided funds or grants to enhance their students' learning in reading. There are many resources and books that are directly related to reading state standards and benchmarks. Similarly, workloads can be split up amongst members of the team. Rather than each teacher finding materials for several standards, each member of the team can locate materials for a specific standard with which the majority of the team's students struggle.

Some schools employ a **reading coach** who specializes in ELA and content standards. A primary role of reading coaches is to be trained in reading interventions in order to provide teachers the strategies needed to ensure their students meet annual growth expectations of select benchmarks. In order to become specialists in such reading processes, reading coaches attend district-wide meetings to learn about resources, strategies, and curriculum changes. Reading coaches are great advocates when it comes to getting resources. They help schools and/or districts select texts, leveled readers, and matching assessments. Reading coaches also train and educate teachers in how to use such resources effectively within their classrooms. Sometimes, reading coaches even teach lessons, help with small groups, or assess students.

Promoting Independent Reading in the Classroom and at Home

It is important to set times for independent reading in the classroom. Letting students choose their own books to read by themselves allows them to read about subjects that interest them in a stress-free setting.

Book clubs are also a way for students to practice independent reading. There are a number of ways to incorporate these clubs. For example, a teacher could break the class into groups by interest, ask the members of each group to read a book at home, and then have students gather during class time to discuss their reading assignment. For a more informal approach to a book club, a teacher could encourage students to voluntarily participate in a club. Depending on the age and level of the students, the teacher's involvement in this club could be anything from direct leadership (picking the books,

leading the discussions, etc.) to indirect supervision (giving students suggestions for which books to pick, answering questions about the material, etc.).

Additionally, **reading challenges** are a good way to encourage students to read by themselves. For example, you might have students record how many pages they read during a week or two and offer prizes for children who read more than a given number of pages. Although you can always organize reading challenges for your own class, you can also coordinate with coworkers or the community. School-wide reading challenges can be a fun way to build community as well as reading skills, and many libraries offer reading challenges. External reading challenges, such as those hosted by libraries or other organizations, are particularly useful during school breaks. They are also good for teachers who are already too busy with work because the teacher simply has to tell students about the challenge and encourage them to participate instead of taking the time to create and run it.

Finally, the teacher modeling a positive attitude toward independent reading motivates students to invest time in it themselves. If a teacher complains about reading or otherwise makes it seem like a chore, they cannot expect the students to display a better attitude. However, by emphasizing how interesting and fun reading is, teachers can inspire a passion for reading in their students.

Instructional Technologies to Promote Reading Development

Although technology can be distracting and overstimulating, using it in some contexts can help students build reading skills and boost engagement.

Teaching vocabulary is one area in which technology is particularly useful. Often, teachers need to make their own materials while teaching vocabulary nonelectronically. This preparation can be a long process of looking up definitions, gathering images, etc. However, there are many digital programs that teach vocabulary through included pictures and pronunciation guides. These can be valuable resources because they teach vocabulary in a visual and engaging way. Additionally, many digital texts allow students to see the definition of a word by hovering the cursor over it or clicking on it. This kind of tool allows students to learn new words almost instantly when they encounter them, which aids comprehension and helps students who would not be motivated enough to look up the word if it was difficult or time-consuming.

Digital flash cards can be a good way to drill letters and the sounds they make. For example, some programs allow children to see a letter, say the sound, and then click on the card to hear the sound it makes and check themselves.

There are also many programs that allow the student to listen to the text and read it at the same time. These programs are good for developing reading fluency in children who struggle with blending or are reading with a strange intonation because the audio gives them a smooth reader to imitate. However, teachers should not overuse this type of program, particularly with young or beginning students, because trying to keep up with the audio may cause them to focus on speed rather than accuracy and become sloppy readers.

When using technology in the classroom, teachers should be aware that not all students are equally familiar with technology. Students' ability to use technology depends on many things, from their families' socioeconomic status to personal preferences. Clearly, a student who is growing up using computers and tablets every day is initially going to be better at navigating educational technology than a student who has only used a computer at the library. Instead of simply assuming their students know

how to use technology, teachers should be available to answer questions and teach students how to use the programs. Otherwise, some students will have a considerable disadvantage during technical work.

Strategies and Resources for Supporting Individual Students

When teaching English-language learners, teachers should make sure they are allowing adequate time for teaching language acquisition. If a student is a raw beginner and there is not enough time to teach foundation principles in your classroom, find supplemental programs for the student in your school or community. Unless the student is extremely young (preschool or kindergarten), do not expect them to easily fit in with the rest of the class. It is helpful to be aware of your students' language backgrounds so you can anticipate the struggles they face. For example, a student who grew up reading Cyrillic may find the English phonetic writing system familiar but struggle with letters such as *h*, which exists in both alphabets but makes different sounds. On the other hand, a student who can already read Hebrew would have no competing ideas about the alphabet sounds but might have difficulty tracking because they are used to reading from right to left.

Like English-language learners, struggling readers can benefit from supplemental programs. Many schools and communities offer intervention programs for readers who are at risk for falling behind grade level or have already done so, and sending students to these classes can help them catch up. Multisensory education is also a great way to help struggling students. Often, students have difficulty reading because their learning styles are unlike those of other students. A student who learns best through movement, for instance, will struggle if they are being taught through visual and auditory methods. Additionally, some students simply need more repetition, and receiving information through multiple pathways provides that repetition. Using multisensory strategies, such as acting out stories or making letters out of clay, can help these types of student internalize concepts through different neural pathways and fully engage with the material.

Finally, highly proficient readers are at risk for becoming bored in class and losing their motivation to work. These students generally do best when they are given as much choice as possible and supported when they pursue their passions. You could help a gifted student who loves physics find books about the subject and then talk about the books with the student after they have read them. It can also be helpful to connect these students with other people who share their interests or skills, in or outside of the school. For example, you could help a high-achieving student become involved in programs for gifted students, join competitions larger than those offered in your school, or find professional mentors. In addition, you can offer supplemental reading and projects for accelerated students, such as giving all students an optional assignment of reading a book related to your lesson. Students who finish their work quickly or are especially interested in the subject could further their learning by completing this extra project.

Response to Intervention (RTI) Process

Response to Intervention Process (RTI) is a process designed to help struggling students catch up through intervention and monitoring in a general education classroom. Students who suffer from undiagnosed reading disorders, attention issues, or even ELL students struggling to learn the language may begin to fall behind the rest of the students in reading skills. RTI is an informal intervention process done by the school that focuses on utilizing research and technology to help the student "catch up" to the rest of the class. The school's RTI teams will review assessments taken of each child in the classroom to determine which students need these instructional interventions. Teachers track students through **progress monitoring**, a process that measures whether or not the interventions are making a difference.

Subarea III—Reading Assessment and Instruction

Although there are various ways to do RTI, it is usually set up as a three-tier system of support, also known as **multi-tier system of supports** (MTSS). The tiers below are in order of least intense to most intense:

Tier 1: High-Quality Classroom Instruction, Screening, and Group Interventions

In Tier 1 interventions, the entire classroom is assessed using **universal screening**, where everyone's skillset is measured in a general education classroom using methods that have been proven to be effective. Students who receive Tier 1 support are generally divided into small groups based on their skill level. Many students receive Tier 1 support because their math or reading skills are not quite at grade level. Progress of Tier 1 instruction is monitored, and many students are able to catch up to grade level effectively.

Tier 2: Targeted Interventions

Tier 2 interventions are **targeted interventions** that take place outside of regular classroom time and give more detailed attention to the struggling student. These may be conducted during extracurricular activities or electives.

Tier 3: Intensive Interventions and Comprehensive Evaluation

The third tier of the RTI process is **intensive intervention**. Intensive interventions are often done one-on-one or in small groups with other special-needs children. Usually only one or two students in a classroom will need this kind of instruction, so one-on-one help is more readily available for this tier.

This material is provided for exam preparation purposes only and does not indicate an endorsement of any specific scientific, political, or religious point of view. © TPB Publishing. You have been licensed one copy of this document for personal use only. Any other reproduction or redistribution is strictly prohibited. All rights reserved.

Practice Quiz

1. Which of the following is NOT true in Tier 1 interventions?
   a. The entire classroom is assessed using universal screening.
   b. Students who receive Tier 1 support are generally given one-on-one support in addition to classroom teaching.
   c. Progress of Tier 1 instruction is monitored, and many students are able to catch up to grade level effectively.
   d. Many students receive Tier 1 support because their math or reading skills are not quite at grade level.

2. Ability-based differentiation involves which of the following core focus areas?
   a. How students sound out unfamiliar words
   b. How students analyze and use a reading
   c. How students self-select appropriately leveled readings
   d. How students work in peer groups

3. A student takes a standardized formal reading assessment and achieves a score that lands them in the 77th percentile. What does this mean?
   a. The student answered 77% of the questions correctly.
   b. The student answered 77 questions correctly.
   c. The student performed better than 77% of test takers.
   d. 77 percent of test takers scored higher than the student.

4. If diagnostic assessments indicate students have phonetic problems, which of the following activities would be best for the instructor to introduce?
   a. Activities that analyze the different aspects of words.
   b. Activities that help students visualize what they read.
   c. Activities that have students paraphrase and summarize texts.
   d. Activities that involve using graphic organizers to identify key points and supporting details in texts.

5. Which of the following is an example of interest-based differentiation?
   a. Grouping students who are all struggling with comprehending grade-level vocabulary words.
   b. Grouping students who are all working on reading fluency.
   c. Grouping students who are all working on sounding out unfamiliar words when reading aloud.
   d. Grouping students who are all auditory learners.

See answers on the next page.

Answer Explanations

1. B: Rather than receiving primarily one-on-one support, students who receive Tier 1 support are generally divided into small groups based on their skill level. One-on-one support is more characteristic of Tier 3 support because this format can provide a more intensive intervention.

2. D: Ability-based differentiation addresses three core areas of focus that determine reading proficiency and build reading skills. These include examining students' conceptual understanding of reading, how students analyze and use the reading, and how students evaluate and respond to reading. The other choices describe important skills that students develop, but they are not hallmarks of ability-based differentiation.

3. C: Percentile scores provide a means of score comparisons and range from 1 to 99. A student's percentile score indicates the percentage of total test takers that student outperformed. For example, a student who scored in the 77th percentile achieved a score that is higher than 77% of the rest of the test cohort. A student's percentile score is different than the percentage of correct responses obtained on the test. A percentile score simply compares one student's score with the scores of all of the other students who took the test.

4. A: When students have phonetic problems, instructors should introduce activities that help the students sound out words and analyze their different aspects to build familiarity with English vocabulary and structure. The other choices would be more appropriate activities to aid reading comprehension.

5. D: Interest-based differentiation is based on the concept that students' performance can be associated with their interest level in the subject or activity. Choices *A, B*, and *C* are based on performance or skill level, while Choice *D* is an example of interest-based differentiation. Instructors can encourage reading growth by allowing students to choose their learning activities. Students more interested in auditory activities may find listening to oral reading exercises more engaging than reading alone in their own head.

Subarea IV—Integration of Knowledge and Understanding

Foundational Reading Skills

Prepare an Organized Written Response to a Case Study of an Elementary Student

A **case study** is a formal written analysis that has a clear overarching purpose. A case study on an individual elementary student focuses on the individual in question and examines their learning issues and progress throughout instruction. The case study documents specific reading issues and solutions in order to learn from this individual study to help future instructors and students. It's also crucial to have a clear timeline of progress throughout the study.

Case studies should open with the student's reading issues. A candidate should explain where the difficulties occurred, such as in speaking challenges, reading struggles, and poor results on assessments. This establishes the focus of the study to help the student overcome issues by improving instruction. Sometimes, there are no issues to solve in a study. If this is the case, a study can focus on new teaching strategies, such as the introduction of a new study resource or lesson structure. In this scenario, the candidate should begin with why the new methods are being applied and the goals of these new strategies—perhaps to improve reading instruction while boosting class engagement.

After introducing the root problem or question of the case study, there needs to be data. Candidates should document the steps taken to address the causes of the issues. Describing the methodologies used for pinpointing specific areas of reading confusion will clarify where and why the issues are occurring. From here, it's time to document the prescribed instruction modifications used to get the student up to speed. In addition to writing how and why differentiated instruction was used to help the student, the candidate should also describe the results of teaching alterations. If the first round of differentiated instruction doesn't help, the instructor should describe this and then explore why this was so. The writer should also discuss how teaching methods then changed again to become more effective. When new instruction takes effect and the student improves, the outcome should also be written about to clearly Illustrate the results. Improvements are very important in these case studies and will help establish successful methods for future reading instruction.

Organizing a Written Response to a Topic Relating to Student Literacy

In addition to researching new education methods and discoveries, reading specialist candidates should be comfortable writing about their field. Whether it's new research, an analysis of a particular class, or a status report, it's important to utilize good writing skills. The writing should be detailed and yet as concise as possible. Using clear, easy-to-understand language will ensure that all readers will be able to grasp the material properly. It's important to focus on the specific subject matter at hand and not deviate; instead, reading specialists should elaborate on relevant points and why they matter.

When writing about student literacy, it's important to distinguish research or accepted views, observations, and opinions. Just like with a student's composition, any claim made regarding the profession of literary instruction should be corroborated with supporting information. For example, if there is a specific learning disability being addressed, it would be useful to describe specific indications of this issue and how this impacts the cognition of reading. Then, after establishing this base

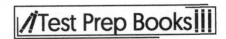

information, an instructor can describe its relevance—how it applies to their current work. Providing detailed observations will also be useful.

When documenting observations, it is important to not only note key areas of difficulty or potential learning disorders but also strategies for improvement. Providing a plan of how to address these issues will enable the instructor to learn appropriate teaching methods and set goals for the student. Assessment results can be documented as well. By showing successive assessments, the writer can illustrate patterns that indicate reading issues and/or show student progress after differentiated instruction.

Analyzing core issues in literacy development shows an in-depth knowledge of how reading is learned in relation to adolescent cognition. To do this effectively, candidates should be able to address the stages of development and assess a student's current stage. Addressing other concepts, such as the effect of culture and perspective, can also play a role in responses. These are also factors that can cause misinterpretation of reading materials or simply produce an alternate interpretation. Therefore, these differences should be elaborated on to eliminate any confusion.

Reading Comprehension

Teaching Students to Read Informational Texts

Here are some strategies for teaching students to understand and analyze informational texts.

Before the class reads a text, give students a few guiding questions and ask them to find the answers in the reading. For example, suppose that your students are about to read a book about the salmon lifecycle. You might ask them, "How many times do salmon travel during their lives?" and "Where do salmon die?" Approaching the text with guiding questions helps structure students' thoughts and teaches them to take notes. This method is particularly useful for young students, as it takes the attention off the unimportant details that sometimes fascinate young readers and redirects it to the central points of the text.

Teach students to summarize information. For example, you could ask students to take notes on the most important points in a text and then write a summary. Younger students do better with simple oral summaries, while older students can handle more complicated written work. Summarizing is a great way to improve comprehension. It also tests analysis skills, as students need to discern which points are important and which are just details.

Ask students to develop questions about the text. For instance, you could ask each student to read the assigned text and then bring one question about it to class. Teaching students to generate questions helps them be curious about reading and promotes creative thinking. This is particularly helpful when teaching older students to analyze more complex texts, as it teaches them to form arguments and evaluate material. For example, tenth graders could read a persuasive text and then bring questions that challenge its claims.

Teach students to form connections between the text and other material. For instance, students could read one book about Russia and another about Spain and then compare the two countries.

Alternatively, teachers can ask students to draw comparisons between the information in a text and their life experiences. This method is particularly effective for younger students, as it boosts

engagement. For example, after reading a book about beavers, a teacher might ask their students whether any of them has seen a beaver. The class could then compare the information in the book to the students' experiences.

Teaching Literary Texts

While the strategies for teaching literary texts often overlap with those for teaching informational texts, there are a few key differences.

While guiding questions are just as helpful for literature as for informational texts, the questions for literary texts can be more open-ended and offer opportunities for students to express opinions on the reading. For example, teachers can ask questions like "Do you think the character makes the right decision?" or "How does the novel's setting contribute to the plot?" Teach students to engage with the material and back up their claims.

Teach students to support their analysis of literature with textual evidence. **Textual evidence** is material from the literary text itself. A student who bases an argument on historical facts, the author's life, or personal experience is not using textual evidence; however, someone who argues from the events and wording of a novel is using textual evidence. Teaching students about textual evidence helps them read closely and learn to form unbiased arguments.

Teach students to map stories and identify literary elements. **Freytag's pyramid** is the most common method of mapping the critical developments in a story. It is particularly useful for helping students understand the important events in a novel. For example, you could have students map *To Kill a Mockingbird* individually, and then discuss the maps as a class. Students should also know terms like "setting" and "theme" so that they can talk and write about their ideas.

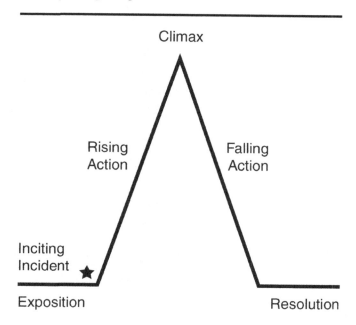

Freytag Pyramid

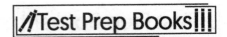

While there are correct and incorrect answers to questions about the factual events in a literary text, the answers to questions about themes and the text's message are not so simple. Instead of offering definitive readings on what the text means, facilitate discussion and make suggestions. Studying literature is a great way for students to develop creativity and argumentative skills, and you do not want to squelch that process by being too authoritative.

Sample Open-Response

Prepare an Organized Written Response to Instruct Teachers on What Process to Use.

Scenario: Mr. Brown is a reading specialist at Carroll High School and assists several teachers and classes with literacy development skills. While most students seem to be writing well, Mr. Brown notices that several students in the classes seem to have trouble reading written words. These children come from a wide range of backgrounds, including native and non-native English speakers.

Task 1: What are some ways Mr. Brown can assess the students' skill levels to determine where the root of their reading issues lie?

Task 2: Describe how Mr. Brown can guide the instructors in addressing the reading issues with differentiated instruction.

Practice Test

Multiple-Choice Questions

1. Which of the following is an essential component of effective reading fluency?
   a. Reading rate
   b. Genre of text
   c. Size of print
   d. Background knowledge

2. When does scaffolded reading occur?
   a. A student hears a recording of herself reading a text in order to set personal reading goals.
   b. A student receives assistance and feedback on strategies to utilize while reading.
   c. A student is given extra time to find the answers to predetermined questions.
   d. A student is pulled out of a class to receive services elsewhere.

3. Which of the following about effective independent reading is NOT true?
   a. Students should read texts that are below their reading levels during independent reading.
   b. Students need to demonstrate fluency before reading independently.
   c. Students who don't yet display automaticity should whisper to themselves when reading aloud.
   d. Students who demonstrate automaticity in decoding should be held accountable during independent reading.

4. Timed oral reading can be used to assess which of the following?
   a. Phonics
   b. Listening comprehension
   c. Reading rate
   d. Background knowledge

5. Syntax is best described as what?
   a. The arrangement of words into sentences
   b. The study of language meaning
   c. The study of grammar and language structure
   d. The proper formatting of a written text

6. What are the three interconnected indicators of reading fluency?
   a. Phonetics, word morphology, and listening comprehension
   b. Accuracy, rate, and prosody
   c. Syntax, semantics, and vocabulary
   d. Word exposure, phonetics, and decodable skills

7. When building a class library, a teacher should be cognizant of the importance of what?
   a. Providing fiction that contains concepts relating to the background knowledge of all students in the class.
   b. Utilizing only nonfiction text that correlates to state and national standards in order to reinforce academic concept knowledge.
   c. Utilizing a single genre of text in order to reduce confusion of written structures.
   d. Including a wide range of fiction and nonfiction texts at multiple reading levels.

120

8. Samantha is in second grade and struggles with fluency. Which of the following strategies is likely to be most effective in improving Samantha's reading fluency?
    a. The teacher prompts Samantha when she pauses upon coming across an unknown word.
    b. The teacher records Samantha as she reads aloud.
    c. The teacher reads a passage out loud several times to Samantha and then has Samantha read the same passage.
    d. The teacher uses read-alouds and verbalizes contextual strategies that can be used to identify unfamiliar words.

9. Poetry is often an effective device when teaching what skill?
    a. Fluency
    b. Spelling
    c. Writing
    d. Word decoding

10. What do English language learners need to identify prior to comprehending text?
    a. Vocabulary
    b. Figurative language
    c. Author's purpose
    d. Setting

11. Which is NOT a reason why independent reading is important for developing reading comprehension?
    a. It helps students develop a lifelong love of reading.
    b. It encourages students to read a genre they enjoy.
    c. It provides an opportunity for students to read at their own pace.
    d. It gives students time to visit the reading corner, which is an area of the classroom that is restful and enjoyable.

12. Reading fluency is best described as the ability to do what?
    a. Read smoothly and accurately
    b. Comprehend what is read
    c. Demonstrate phonetic awareness
    d. Properly pronounce a list of words

13. Which of the following is the study of what words mean in certain situations?
    a. Morphology
    b. Pragmatics
    c. Syntax
    d. Semantics

14. Why are purposeful read-alouds by a teacher important to enhance reading comprehension?
    a. They encourage students to unwind from a long day and reading lesson.
    b. They encourage students to listen for emphasis and tone.
    c. They encourage students to compare the author's purpose to the teacher's objective.
    d. They encourage students to work on important work from earlier in the day while listening to a story.

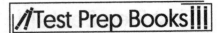

15. What allows readers to effectively translate print into recognizable speech?
    a. Fluency
    b. Spelling
    c. Phonics
    d. Word decoding

16. What does the Yopp-Singer Test evaluate?
    a. Syllabification
    b. Phonics
    c. Phonemic awareness
    d. Sound blending

17. What is the spelling stage of a student who looks at a word and is able to tell the teacher that the letters spell C-A-T, but who cannot actually say the word?
    a. Pre-phonetic State
    b. Transitional Stage
    c. Conventional Stage
    d. Semiphonetic Stage

18. What should be taught and mastered first when teaching reading comprehension?
    a. Theme
    b. Word analysis and fluency
    c. Text evidence
    d. Writing

19. Which of the following is NOT an example of pre-teaching?
    a. Teaching syllabification to students before asking them to complete a worksheet on rhyme meters.
    b. Teaching new vocabulary to students before reading a chapter in a book.
    c. Teaching students how to find and reference a table of contents before using a basal reader in class.
    d. Teaching a history unit on Ancient Egypt before reading a historical fiction novel about a pharaoh.

20. A teacher reads aloud a series of rhyming words and asks the students to identify the rime. What is the teacher doing?
    a. Teaching students how to spell
    b. Explaining homographs
    c. Working with students on identifying morphemes
    d. Helping students with future word decoding

21. Which activity is part of book handling skills in kindergarten?
    a. Being able to read simple words
    b. Summarizing the book after completing it
    c. Turning the pages in the correct order
    d. Identifying pictures

22. As the teacher reads aloud from a book, a student follows the text, which is projected onto a whiteboard and underlined with a pointer. Which skill does this reinforce?
    a. Fluency
    b. Reading environmental print
    c. Automaticity
    d. Tracking print

23. A teacher holds up a picture of the sun and then a picture of a flower. The teacher then has the class say the word "sunflower." What does this activity teach students about?
    a. Syllables
    b. Closed compound words
    c. Morphological awareness
    d. Open compound words

24. A teacher shows students a list of words including *blend*, *blur*, and *blue*. The teacher then pronounces each word, splitting the onset and the rime: *bl end*, *bl ur*, and *bl ue*. What is the primary goal of this activity?
    a. Encourage students to decode words.
    b. Build students' phonemic awareness.
    c. Teach students the schwa sound.
    d. Introduce vowels and consonants.

25. Students are having difficulty understanding and decoding multisyllabic words. What is the best strategy to employ?
    a. Instruction in phonics
    b. Instruction in etymology
    c. Inclusion of intensive reading
    d. Instruction in structural analysis

26. A student has known issues decoding consonant blends. The student makes a mistake when reading the following text out loud: *Halloween is my favorite holiday. Last year, I went as a ghost. This year, I will wear a crown but no mask.* Which reading mistake indicates issues with decoding consonant blends?
    a. Misreading *ghost* as *ghast*
    b. Saying *make* instead of *mask*
    c. Mispronouncing *Halloween*
    d. Adding an *s* to *holiday*

27. A first-grade teacher decides add a writing element to show and tell, where students write a short description of the object they brought and read it aloud, and classmates must guess what it might be before it's revealed. What is NOT one of the possible goals of this exercise?
    a. Change up an activity to challenge the students' thinking.
    b. Challenge the students' descriptive language skills.
    c. Develop the students' written language and listening skills.
    d. Build the students' vocabularies.

123

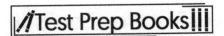

28. A kindergarten teacher posts letters around the classroom and puts several baskets of items in the middle of the room. The teacher has students select an item, say its name, and then put the object near the sign that represents the letter it starts with. What is this activity doing?
   a. Introducing morphemes
   b. Connecting phonemes to letters
   c. Introducing onset and rime
   d. Practicing literary analysis

29. What is the primary goal of lessons in root words and etymology?
   a. Improve kinesthetic learning.
   b. Improve spelling.
   c. Improve reading fluency.
   d. Improve students' decoding and vocabulary skills.

30. In the word *shut*, the *sh* is an example of what?
   a. Consonant digraph
   b. Sound segmentation
   c. Vowel digraph
   d. Rime

31. When students identify the phonemes in spoken words, they are practicing which of the following?
   a. Sound blending
   b. Substitution
   c. Rhyming
   d. Segmentation

32. What is the alphabetic principle?
   a. The understanding that letters represent sounds in words
   b. The ability to combine letters to correctly spell words
   c. The proper use of punctuation within writing
   d. The memorization of all the letters in the alphabet

33. The study of roots, suffixes, and prefixes is called what?
   a. Listening comprehension
   b. Word consciousness
   c. Word morphology
   d. Textual analysis

34. Print awareness includes all EXCEPT which of the following concepts?
   a. The differentiation of uppercase and lowercase letters
   b. The identification of word boundaries
   c. The proper tracking of words
   d. The spelling of sight words

35. When teachers point to words during shared readings, what are they modeling?
   I. Word boundaries
   II. Directionality
   III. One-to-one correspondence

   a. I and II
   b. I and III
   c. II and III
   d. I, II, and III

36. Structural analysis would be the most appropriate strategy in determining the meaning of which of the following words?
   a. Extra
   b. Improbable
   c. Likely
   d. Wonder

37. A student spells *eagle* as *EGL*. This student is performing at which stage of spelling?
   a. Conventional
   b. Phonetic
   c. Semiphonetic
   d. Transitional

38. A kindergarten student is having difficulty distinguishing the letters *b* and *d*. The teacher should do which of the following?
   a. Have the student use a think-aloud to verbalize the directions of the shapes used when writing each letter.
   b. Have the student identify the letters within grade-appropriate texts.
   c. Have the student write each letter five times.
   d. Have the student write a sentence in which all of the letters start with either *b* or *d*.

39. When differentiating phonics instruction for English-language learners (ELLs), teachers should do which of the following?
   a. Increase the rate of instruction.
   b. Begin with the identification of word boundaries.
   c. Focus on syllabication.
   d. Capitalize on the transfer of relevant skills from the learners' original language(s).

40. The identification of morphemes within words occurs during the instruction of what?
   a. Structural analysis
   b. Syllabic analysis
   c. Phonics
   d. The alphabetic principle

41. Which of the following pairs of words are homophones?
   a. Playful and replay
   b. To and too
   c. Was and were
   d. Gloomy and sad

125

42. Spelling instruction should include which of the following?
   I. Word walls
   II. Daily reading opportunities
   III. Daily writing opportunities

   a. I and II
   b. I, II, and III
   c. I and III
   d. II and III

43. Nursery rhymes are used in kindergarten to develop what?
   a. Print awareness
   b. Phoneme recognition
   c. Syllabication
   d. Structural analysis

44. What ability is a key element of reading fluency?
   a. The ability to read English when it is not your first language
   b. The ability to read automatically, recognizing words through subconscious phonetic processes
   c. The ability to read without making mistakes
   d. The ability to self-correct and move on when you make mistakes in your reading

45. The Directed Reading Thinking Activity (DRTA) method helps students to do what?
   a. Build prior knowledge by exploring audiovisual resources before a reading
   b. Predict what will occur in a text and search the text to verify the predictions
   c. Identify, define, and review unfamiliar terms
   d. Understand the format of multiple types and genres of text

46. How are typographic features useful when teaching reading comprehension?
   a. Typographic features are graphics used to illustrate the story and help students visualize the text.
   b. Typographic features give the answers in boldfaced print.
   c. Typographic features are not helpful when teaching reading comprehension and should not be used.
   d. Typographic features such as boldface, italics, and subheadings can be used to highlight important vocabulary or content or indicate changes in topics.

47. What is "text evidence" when referring to answering a comprehension question?
   a. Taking phrases directly from the text itself to answer a question
   b. Using a variety of resources to find the answer
   c. Using technology and websites to locate an answer
   d. Paraphrasing and using a student's own words to answer the question

48. Which of the following is the MOST important reason why group-based discussions in the classroom enhance reading comprehension?
    a. They promote student discussions without the teacher present.
    b. They promote student discussions with a friend.
    c. They promote student discussions so that those who didn't understand the text can get answers from another student.
    d. They give all students a voice and allow them to share their answers, rather than one student sharing an answer with the class.

49. What is a phoneme?
    a. A word
    b. A relationship between a letter and a sound
    c. An individual sound
    d. A consonant

50. A teacher who provides a connection between an English language learner's cultural background and new vocabulary is using which strategy?
    a. Scaffolding
    b. Collaboration
    c. Discourse
    d. Relevance

51. A teacher who creates lessons around prefixes is teaching which vocabulary acquisition strategy?
    a. Contextual analysis
    b. Etymological analysis
    c. Morphemic analysis
    d. Inferential analysis

52. A teacher has two groups of students. One group is instructed to complete the reading and write down any words they do not know. The other group is provided with a list of vocabulary words to define prior to the reading. The group provided with the list is most likely struggling with which of the following?
    a. Spelling
    b. Automaticity
    c. Dictionary use
    d. Comprehension

53. When a student looks back at a previous reading section for information, he or she is using which of the following?
    a. Self-monitoring comprehension
    b. KWL charts
    c. Metacognitive skills
    d. Directed reading-thinking activities

127

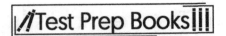

54. A teacher is planning a reading assignment with a complex subject matter. To improve reading comprehension, which strategy should the teacher focus on first?
    a. Identifying and defining new vocabulary
    b. Discussing historical context of the text after reading
    c. Utilizing pre-reading techniques such as SQ3R
    d. Review strategies for contextual clues to determine meaning

55. As an extensive reading exercise, a teacher sets aside 45 minutes once a week to allow students to read a chapter book or novel that is at or below their grade level. What is the teacher trying to do?
    a. Increase fluency
    b. Increase comprehension
    c. Increase vocabulary
    d. Increase automaticity

56. After reading a short story, students are asked to summarize the story and its main plot points. Which level of understanding is involved?
    a. Inferential
    b. Literal
    c. Evaluative
    d. Analytical

57. When introducing literary response, what kind of stories should the teacher choose?
    a. Stories connected to student experiences
    b. Stories that are easy to read
    c. Stories that include new vocabulary words
    d. Stories that use academic language

58. A list of vocabulary words pulled from a social studies textbook is an example of:
    a. Non-contextual vocabulary strategy
    b. Intensive reading strategy
    c. Contextual vocabulary strategy
    d. Transferable vocabulary lesson

59. A student is pre-reading a chapter in a textbook. Which element would be the most useful for the student's attempt to figure out the subject matter of the chapter in pre-reading?
    a. Section headings
    b. Images
    c. End questions
    d. Chapter title

60. An eighth-grade class is preparing to read *The Diary of Anne Frank*. Which activity should the students do to best prepare them for understanding this text?
    a. Writing a diary about a day in their own life
    b. Writing down what they think the book might be about
    c. Learning something about the historical background of World War II
    d. Watching the movie version of *The Diary of Anne Frank*

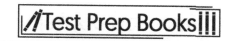

61. What is the method called that teachers use before and after reading to improve critical thinking and comprehension?
   a. Self-monitoring comprehension
   b. KWL charts
   c. Metacognitive skills
   d. Directed reading-thinking activities

62. A sixth-grade teacher gives students an informational text about a historical event and a set of questions to answer. The teacher instructs students to read the questions before beginning the text. Why is that valuable?
   a. It prepares students for unfamiliar vocabulary.
   b. It prepares students for the information and guides them to key elements.
   c. It prepares students to read academic language.
   d. It prepares student to develop their own questions regarding the text.

63. After reading a short story, the teacher introduces the idea of literary response. This is the students' first time encountering the activity. What should the teacher ask the students to do?
   a. Discuss the themes of the story and their importance.
   b. Name and describe the characters.
   c. Summarize the story and main plot points.
   d. Comment on what the text makes them think about in their own lives.

64. While reading a story, students come across the phrase "spill the beans." To help the students understand this idiom, what should the teacher do?
   a. Instruct students to look up the words in a dictionary.
   b. Have students make up their own story about what it means.
   c. Share other idioms about food.
   d. Talk about the history of beans.

65. When introducing students to foreign words used in the English language, what is a useful technique?
   a. Organize the words by theme.
   b. Co-teach a lesson with a foreign language teacher.
   c. Write a list of foreign words on the board and let students decode them.
   d. Assign students a country and have them look for words from that country.

66. A teacher puts orange cones in a field. There is a word on each cone. Students must run to the cone and read the word before they can move to the next. This activity appeals to which kind of learner?
   a. Auditory learners
   b. English Language Learners
   c. Visual learners
   d. Kinesthetic learners

67. A teacher is constructing a list of vocabulary words for their class. The students are starting their first chapter book soon. What kind of words should the teacher select?
   a. A mix of known and unknown words
   b. Words that students will see only in the book
   c. Words that will help students comprehend the book
   d. Words that are not in the book but that the students need to know

68. What is the primary goal of having students do intensive reading?
    a. Encourage students to interact with the text.
    b. Teach students how to use reference books.
    c. Foster vocabulary, syntax, and context clue skills.
    d. Prepare students for literary analysis.

69. Which is the largest contributor to the development of students' written vocabulary?
    a. Extensive reading
    b. Directed reading
    c. Direct teaching
    d. Modeling

70. A student is able to draw connections between a text and their background knowledge. What level of comprehension is this student displaying?
    a. Literal comprehension
    b. Inferential comprehension
    c. Evaluative comprehension
    d. Integrated comprehension

71. What is a guiding question?
    a. A question followed by an answer so students can check their work
    b. A rhetorical question that makes students think deeply
    c. A question a student invents for himself or herself
    d. A question given before the reading or lesson to help students look for important information

72. Which of the following are important skills for the close reading of informational texts?
    a. Evaluating the author's logic and evidence; distinguishing facts from beliefs
    b. Identifying literary devices such as alliteration; recognizing point of view
    c. Distinguishing facts from beliefs; mapping the plot
    d. Recognizing point of view; evaluating characterization and setting

73. Which of the following is NOT a valid use of a reading strategy?
    a. Claire wants to find out whether an article will be a relevant source for her essay, so she scans/skims it for keywords.
    b. Grace reads *Harry Potter* for pleasure, and she reads it so fast that she does not remember some minor characters' names.
    c. Sam is a struggling reader, so he scans/skims the novel his class is reading for important facts.
    d. Terry wants to compare two descriptions of historical events, so he cross-references them.

74. Cassy asks her students to write down three questions about their assignment, try their best to create answers, and bring them to class. What technique is Cassy teaching her students?
    a. Retelling
    b. Self-questioning
    c. Evaluative thinking
    d. Guiding questions

75. A student draws the following diagram:

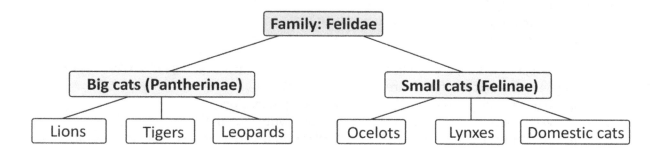

What comprehension strategy is the student using?
- a. Structure charting
- b. Outlining
- c. Chronological arrangement
- d. Semantic mapping

76. Which of the following are correct descriptions?
  I. Text features are textual elements that fall outside the main text, such as indexes and glossaries.
  II. Graphic features are the ways in which a text is laid out, such as paragraphs and headings.
  III. Text features are literary devices, such as similes and metaphors.
  IV. Graphic features are visual elements that supplement the main text, such as charts, graphs, and timelines.

- a. I and II
- b. II and IV
- c. I and IV
- d. II and III

77. Cassandra wants to teach comprehension strategies through modeling. Which of the following steps should she take?
- a. Asking students to share ideas about the text
- b. Encouraging students to draw and map the text visually
- c. Explaining her own thought process as she analyzes a text
- d. Having students discuss the text in small groups

78. Andrea encourages her students to think about their own thoughts and learning processes so they can find learning strategies that work for them. What is Andrea teaching her students?
- a. Metacognition
- b. Self-questioning
- c. Mind maps
- d. Self-regulation

79. What contributes the MOST to schema development?
    a. Reading comprehension
    b. Structural analysis
    c. Written language
    d. Background knowledge

80. A teacher assigns a writing prompt in order to assess her students' reading skills. Which of the following can be said about this form of reading assessment?
    a. It is the most beneficial way to assess reading comprehension.
    b. It is invalid because a student's ability to read and write are unrelated.
    c. It is erroneous since the strength of a student's reading and writing vocabulary may differ.
    d. It is the worst way to assess reading comprehension.

81. What do informal reading assessments allow that standardized reading assessments do NOT allow?
    a. The application of grade-level norms toward a student's reading proficiency
    b. The personalization of reading assessments in order to differentiate instruction
    c. The avoidance of partialities in the interpretation of reading assessments
    d. The comparison of an individual's reading performance to that of other students in the class

82. A teacher needs to assess students' accuracy in reading high frequency sight words and irregular sight words that are grade-appropriate. Which of the following strategies would be most appropriate for this purpose?
    a. The teacher gives students a list of words to study for a spelling test that will be administered the following week.
    b. The teacher allows students to bring their favorite books from home and has them read their selected text aloud independently.
    c. The teacher selects a grade-appropriate text and has each student read the same text aloud independently.
    d. The teacher records how many words each student reads correctly when reading aloud a list of teacher-selected, grade-appropriate words.

83. Which of the following best describes differentiated instruction?
    a. Teaching many different subjects depending on the interests of each student.
    b. Tailoring lessons to meet the different learning styles of different students.
    c. Breaking students up into smaller groups.
    d. Using a wide variety of learning resources in the classroom.

84. What is a summative assessment?
    a. A formal assessment that is given at the end of a unit of study
    b. An informal assessment that is given at the end of a unit of study
    c. An assessment that is given daily and is usually only a few questions in length, based on the day's objective
    d. An assessment given at the end of the week that is usually based on observation

85. What kind of assessment is most beneficial for students with special needs?
    a. Frequent and ongoing
    b. Weekly
    c. Monthly
    d. Summative assessments

86. Which of the following is the most appropriate assessment of spelling for students who are performing at the pre-phonetic stage?
    a. Sight word drills
    b. Phonemic awareness tests
    c. Writing samples
    d. Concepts about print (CAP) test

87. Phonological awareness is best assessed through which of the following?
    a. Identification of rimes or onsets within words
    b. Identification of letter-sound correspondences
    c. Comprehension of an audio book
    d. Writing samples

88. High-frequency words such as *be, the*, and *or* are taught during the instruction of what?
    a. Phonics skills
    b. Sight word recognition
    c. Vocabulary development
    d. Structural analysis

89. To thoroughly assess students' phonics skills, teachers should administer assessments that require students to do which of the following?
    a. Decode in context only
    b. Decode in isolation only
    c. Both A and B
    d. Neither A nor B

90. A student is having difficulty pronouncing a word that she comes across when reading aloud. Which of the following is most likely NOT a reason for the difficulty that the student is experiencing?
    a. Poor word recognition
    b. A lack of content vocabulary
    c. Inadequate background knowledge
    d. Repeated readings

91. Which of the following would be the best situation for using an annotated digital text?
    a. The students are having difficulty tracking and are skipping passages.
    b. The text has many new vocabulary words.
    c. The text has few paragraph breaks.
    d. The text is self-contained and does not require reference material.

92. Krista takes the Informal Reading Inventory, and she reads a text with 75% accuracy. What is her reading level for that text?
    a. Independent level
    b. Instructional level
    c. Frustration level
    d. Hearing comprehension level

133

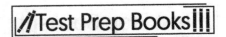

93. What is the difference between validity and reliability?
    a. Validity means the number of questions in a test (more questions mean more valid results); reliability refers to its ability to produce the same results over multiple tests.
    b. Validity means a test's ability to produce the same results over multiple tests; reliability refers to its ability to reflect students' learning accurately.
    c. Validity means a test's ability to reflect students' learning accurately; reliability refers to its ability to produce the same results over multiple tests.
    d. Validity means a test's ability to produce the same results over multiple tests; reliability refers to the number of questions (more questions mean more reliable results).

94. Which of the following is an ideal situation for individual testing?
    a. The teacher wants to find individual students' strengths and weaknesses and encourage them.
    b. The teacher wants to measure the same competencies in every student.
    c. The teacher is testing eighth graders on their reading comprehension.
    d. The teacher is testing fifth graders' cursive skills.

95. What is the Lexile Text Measure?
    a. A readability formula
    b. A way of teaching spelling
    c. A leveling system
    d. A note-taking strategy

96. What is decodable text?
    a. Text that separates the syllables so students can read it more easily
    b. Text that is curated to have only the letters or words students have learned
    c. Text that is broken into short paragraphs so students are not overwhelmed
    d. Digital text that includes definitions for new vocabulary words

97. Carson takes the IRI and scores 60% comprehension and 80% reading accuracy on one passage. What is his reading level for this passage?
    a. Independent level
    b. Instructional level
    c. Frustration level
    d. Hearing capacity level

98. A child is 8 years old, has just learned to understand conservation, and is not yet good at using logic. In which of Piaget's stages is this child?
    a. Sensorimotor
    b. Preoperational
    c. Concrete operational
    d. Formal operational

99. Tony teaches his students phonics, but he also teaches them a few sight words. What approach to reading is Tony using?
    a. The top-down approach
    b. The bottom-up approach
    c. The complementary approach
    d. The integrated approach

100. Why is multisensory education useful?
   a. It creates enough classroom activities to keep the class busy.
   b. It introduces information through multiple pathways.
   c. It prevents children from straining their eyes.
   d. It helps children learn while they are in the sensorimotor stage.

Open-Response Item Assignments

Please write 150–300 words in response to each of the two open-response prompts below. Your response should demonstrate a thorough knowledge of your field and an understanding of both educational principles and how to apply them. The evaluation of your response will be determined by how thoroughly you treat the assignment, your knowledge of the subject and its correct application, the evidence you use to support your argument, and the clarity and depth of your argument. No reference materials are allowed and your response must be original work.

Open-Response Item Assignment #1: Foundational Reading Skills

Use the information below to complete the exercise that follows.

The following case study is focused on Caleb, a second-grade student. Caleb's primary instructor has noticed that when Caleb reads material aloud in class, he will often take long pauses and read the sentences slower than the other students. This sometimes causes him to stutter or hesitate during longer sentences. Another issue is that sometimes he will switch the order of the words he sees, for example, putting the word *the* after the word *cat* in a sentence. Despite this, Caleb is very bright and seems to fully grasp the context of the material. He also appears to be engaged when answering questions but is hesitant when having to read in front of the class. Caleb's teacher has requested that Mr. Breiner, the reading specialist, evaluate Caleb to understand what might be causing his issues. While Caleb is highly intelligent, the teacher is wondering whether his problems with reading may indicate a reading disorder. Mr. Breiner has been requested to present ideas on how to help Caleb's reading skills improve. The teacher wants to be able to learn how to address reading issues like Caleb's in the future, or at least be able to identify core literary issues very early in the developmental stage.

Caleb's teacher gives Mr. Breiner the following notes:

   1. When reading the sentence, "The next-door neighbors adopted the cat that had been homeless," Caleb switched *the* and *cat*. He also seemed to take longer to sound out *homeless*.

   2. Longer sentences seem to cause Caleb confusion when reading aloud.

   3. In some of his writing responses, Caleb will sometimes switch the letters within the words or the words themselves.

   4. Caleb understands material clearly and gives insightful thoughts aloud. No speech problems were observed.

Using your knowledge of **literacy assessment and instructional strategies,** write a response in which you:

• Identify and discuss methods of observation that may indicate whether or not Caleb has a learning disorder. What kind of assessments can be used to determine if his reading difficulties

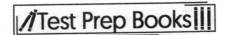
are tied to specific written English structures or if his pausing indicates other psychological disconnects?

- Identify and discuss some teaching strategies that can be used to help Caleb improve. Provide details on why differentiating Caleb's instruction would be a major step in bolstering his reading ability.

Open-Response Item Assignment #2: Reading Comprehension

Use the information below to complete the exercise that follows.

Scenario: The teachers in an elementary school are proactively trying to implement content-area reading instruction in their classrooms. Their goal is to better their students' writing skills and increase comprehension and writing fluency. However, their budget is low, and the implementation must be cost-effective.

Task 1: Briefly provide an example of content-area reading instruction and describe the process in full detail while aligning the process with the budget constraints.

Task 2: Talk about how this instruction will align with an increase in comprehension and writing fluency for the entire school.

Answer Explanations

1. A: Accuracy and reading rate are fundamental components of fluency. Additionally, practice is an essential component of effective fluency instruction. A student's accuracy and rate will likely increase if a teacher provides opportunities to learn words and use word-analysis skills. Oral reading accompanied by guidance and feedback from teachers, peers, or parents has a significant positive impact on fluency. In order to be beneficial, such feedback needs to target specific areas in which students need improvement, as well as strategies that students can use in order to improve in those areas. Such feedback increases students' awareness so that they can independently make needed modifications to improve fluency.

2. B: Scaffolded opportunities occur when a teacher helps students by giving them support, offering immediate feedback, and suggesting strategies. In order to be beneficial, such feedback needs to help students identify areas that need improvement. Much like oral reading feedback, this advice increases students' awareness so they can independently make needed modifications in order to improve fluency.

Scaffolding is lessened as the student becomes a more independent reader. Struggling readers, students with reading difficulties or disabilities, and students with special needs especially benefit from direct instruction and feedback that teaches decoding and analysis of unknown words, automaticity in key sight words, and correct expression and phrasing.

3. A: Once students become fluent readers, independent reading can begin. Students who don't yet display automaticity may need to read out loud or whisper to themselves during independent reading time. Independent silent reading accompanied by comprehension accountability is an appropriate strategy for students who demonstrate automaticity in their decoding skills. Also, each student should be provided with a text that matches their reading level.

4. C: The most common measurement of reading rate includes the oral contextual timed readings of students. During a timed reading, the number of errors made within a given amount of time is recorded. This data can be used to determine if a student's rate is improving and if the rate falls within the recommended range for his or her grade level.

5. A: Syntax refers to the arrangement of words and phrases to form well-developed sentences and paragraphs. Semantics has to do with language meaning. Grammar is a composite of all systems and structures utilized within a language and includes syntax, word morphology, semantics, and phonology. Cohesion and coherence of oral and written language are promoted through a full understanding of syntax, semantics, and grammar.

6. B: Key indicators of reading fluency include accuracy, rate, and prosody. Phonetics and decodable skills aid fluency. Syntax, semantics, word morphology, listening comprehension, and word exposure aid vocabulary development.

7. D: Students within a single classroom come with varied background knowledge, interests, and needs. Thus, it's unrealistic to find texts that apply to all. Students benefit when a wide range of fiction and nonfiction texts are available in a variety of genres, promoting differentiated instruction.

8. D: This answer alludes to both read-alouds and think-alouds. Modeling fluency can be done through read-alouds. Proper pace, phrasing, and expression of text can be modeled when teachers read aloud to their students. During think-alouds, teachers verbalize their thought processes when orally reading a

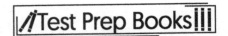

selection. Teachers' explanations may describe strategies they use as they read to monitor their comprehension. In this way, teachers explicitly model the metacognition processes that good readers use to construct meaning from a text.

9. A: The rhythmic sounds and rhyming words of some poems help build a child's phonemic awareness.

10. A: English Language Learners should master vocabulary and word usages in order to fully comprehend text. Figurative language, an author's purpose, and settings are more complex areas and are difficult for English Language Learners. These areas can be addressed once ELL students understand the meanings of words. In order to master comprehension skills, vocabulary and the English language need to be mastered first, but even once vocabulary and English have been mastered, comprehension can still be difficult. Figurative language is culture-based, and inferences may be difficult for those with a different cultural background.

11. D: Although the reading corner should be a restful and enjoyable place to encourage students to read independently, it does not enhance reading comprehension directly. Choices A, B, and C all encourage enhancement of reading comprehension. Giving students a chance to read independently allows them to choose books they enjoy, read at their own pace, and develop a lifelong enjoyment of reading.

12. A: Reading fluency is the ability to accurately read at a socially acceptable pace and with proper expression. Phonetic awareness leads to the proper pronunciation of words and fluency. Once students are able to read fluently, concentration is no longer dedicated toward the process of reading. Instead, students can concentrate on the meaning of a text. Thus, in the developmental process of reading, comprehension follows fluency.

13. B: Pragmatics is the study of what words mean in certain situations. Choice A, morphology, involves the structure and formation of words. Choice C, syntax, refers to the order of words in a sentence. Choice D, semantics, addresses the distinct meanings of words.

14. B: Purposeful teacher read-alouds allow students to listen to a story for voice emphasis and tone. This will help students when they are reading independently as well. Although students may find this time restful or a chance to catch up on old work, neither is the main purpose. Students may use this time to take notes on the reading, but students should only be listening to the story being read and not doing other work.

15. C: Phonics allows readers to effectively translate print into recognizable speech. If children lack proficiency in phonics, their ability to read fluently and to increase vocabulary will be limited.

16. C: The **Yopp-Singer Test of Phonemic Segmentation** is an oral entry-level or summative assessment of phonemic awareness during which a teacher reads twenty-two words aloud one at a time to a single student. Phonemic-aware students recognize specific units of spoken language called phonemes, which are unique and easily identifiable units of sound. Choice A, syllabification, is the dividing of words into their component syllables. Choice B, phonics, is the is the direct correspondence between and blending of letters and sounds. Choice D, sound blending, is the ability to mix together two or more sounds or phonemes. After the Yopp-Singer Test, the blending of words, syllabification, and/or onset-rime identification should be assessed. The last set of phonological and phonemic skills to be assessed is composed of isolation, blending, deletion, and substitution.

138

17. D: During the semiphonetic spelling stage, children can identify the sounds that letters make (the alphabetic principle) but may not be able to blend the individual sounds together to form a word. Choice *A* is incorrect because the pre-phonetic stage is marked by an incomplete understanding of the alphabetic principle and letter-sound correspondences. Choice *B* is incorrect because the transitional stage is a more advanced stage where students have developed a small sight vocabulary and a solid understanding of letter-sound correspondences. Choice *C* is incorrect because the conventional stage is the last spelling stage and occurs when students have a well-developed sight word vocabulary and can read fluently with comprehension.

18. B: Word analysis and fluency should be mastered before teaching theme, text evidence, and writing. For English Language Learners and struggling readers, word analysis and fluency are often difficult barriers, which is why comprehension skills are not initially mastered. Theme is often a complex and inferential skill, which is developed later on. Text evidence is pulling answers to comprehension questions directly from a text and cannot be accomplished until readers can fluently read and understand the text. Writing skills generally come after comprehension skills are underway.

19. A: Choice *A* is an example of teaching a skill and then reinforcing the skill with practice rather than true pre-teaching. Choices *B*, *C*, and *D* are all examples of pre-teaching where necessary skills or background information are taught to students in order to facilitate a separate activity, but the subsequent activities are specifically reinforcing the lesson.

20. D: Choice *D* is correct. The teacher is helping students with future word decoding because the students will begin to recognize the letter patterns through rime. While spelling, Choice *A*, may be a benefit to this kind of activity, it is the sound recognition and the letter pattern that students will recognize, helping them read those same patterns later. Choice *B*, homographs, is incorrect, as homographs are spelled the same but pronounced differently rather than rhyming. Choice *C* is incorrect; morphemes may be included in this activity, but this activity helps more with future word decoding than it does identifying morphemes.

21. C: Choice *C* is correct. Book handling skills are those involved in using a book appropriately. Therefore, turning pages is one of these skills. While Choice *A* suggests that book handling skills are present, reading is not part of book handling skills. Choice *B*, summarizing, is not a book handling skill. Choice *D*, identifying pictures, is also not a book handling skill.

22. D: Choice *D* is correct. When a student is learning to track print, they are watching the teacher read fluently, but they are not actively participating in a way that would reinforce their own reading fluency, so Choice *A* is incorrect. Choice *B* is incorrect; though reading is being modeled, the projected text is not environmental print. Environmental print refers to the words that surround students on an everyday basis, such as advertising and labels. Automaticity, Choice *C*, is reinforced by students reading on their own rather than listening to someone else read, so that is also incorrect. By tracking the print, students are learning and practicing how to follow words across a page and down to the next line.

23. B: Choice *B* is correct. Because the word *flower* has more than one syllable, this wouldn't be a great activity for teaching syllables, so Choice *A* is incorrect. Choice *C* is incorrect; while both parts of the compound words are morphemes, morphological instruction would likely start with smaller words and focus more on the parts of the word rather than the combined result. Choice *D* is incorrect because sunflower is a closed compound word.

24. B: Choice *B* is correct. The point of an activity like this is to introduce or reinforce the sound of the *bl* consonant blend, thus improving phonemic awareness. While a side benefit of this is improving a student's ability to sound out words, Choice *A*, it's not the primary goal here. The sounds in the question are not examples of schwa sounds and the activity is not the best instructional method for teaching those, so Choice *C* is incorrect. Choice *D* is also incorrect; while the words are made up of consonants and vowels, the exercise doesn't isolate them in a way that would be appropriate for the lesson.

25. D: Choice *D* is correct. While phonics, Choice *A*, will help students identify individual sounds, it will likely break the word down into too many parts to enable successful decoding. Etymology, Choice *B*, is a good strategy after the student has decoded a word, to further help them understand it. While intensive reading may introduce multisyllabic words, it's not a great strategy for helping students decode them, so Choice *C* is incorrect. Structural analysis, Choice *D*, teaches students to break down words into known parts such as affixes and root words, enabling them to better decode multisyllabic words.

26. B: Choice *B* is correct. The student is not blending the *s* and *k* sounds to form the word properly and would benefit from work that explores digraphs at the end of words in particular. Choice *A* indicates an issue with vowels, not consonant blends. While Choice *C* includes a double consonant, it does not have a consonant blend. Choice *D* does not involve a blending issue either.

27. D: Choice *D* is the only option that this activity will definitely not achieve. While the activity may introduce some students to new words, it's not likely to contribute significantly to vocabulary acquisition. Changing up an activity, Choice *A*, will definitely challenge students, as will guessing the show and tell items from a brief description. Choice *B* is definitely a goal of this exercise; students will be challenged to describe their objects in ways that make sense to their classmates. Choice *C* is also definitely a goal of this exercise, because it reinforces the connection between spoken and written words for the students

28. B: Choice *B* is correct. This activity directly connects the sound of the name of the object to a letter in the name, thereby connecting sound and letter, or phoneme and letter. Choice *A* and Choice *C* are incorrect. Though morphemes, onset, and rime are all present, this activity doesn't isolate them in a pedagogically valuable way. Choice *D* is incorrect. The activity is not involved in practicing literary analysis.

29. D: Choice *D* is correct. Lessons in root words and etymology help students decode new words and understand their meaning through structural analysis rather than context or by looking up a definition. Choice *A* is incorrect; lessons in root words and etymology does not improve kinesthetic learning. This activity improves spelling, but not as a primary goal, so Choice *B* is incorrect. While eventually a student's ability to conduct structural analysis may improve fluency, it's an outcome of the original goal rather than the goal itself. Further, many of the words students will need to decode will be complex and the decoding means a lack of fluency, so Choice *C* is incorrect.

30. A: The *sh* is an example of a consonant digraph, which is a combination of two consonants that work together to make a single sound. Examples of consonant digraphs are *sh*, *ch*, and *th*. Choice *B*, sound segmentation, is used to identify component phonemes in a word, such as separating the /t/, /u/, and /b/ in tub. Choice *C*, vowel digraph, is a set of two vowels that make up a single sound, such as *ow*, *ae*, or *ie*. Choice *D*, rime, is the sound that follows a word's onset, such as the /at/ in *cat*.

31. D: Phoneme segmentation is the identification of all the component phonemes in a word. An example would be the student identifying each separate sound, /t/, /u/, and /b/, in the word *tub*. Choice

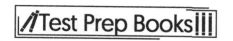

A, sound blending, is the blending together of two or more sounds in a word, such as /ch/ or /sh/. Choice *B*, substitution, occurs when a phoneme is substituted within a word for another phoneme, such as substituting the sound /b/ in *bun* to /r/ to create *run*. Choice *C*, rhyming, is an effective tool to utilize during the analytic phase of phonics development because rhyming words are often identical except for their beginning letters.

32. A: The alphabetic principle is the understanding that letters represent sounds in words. It is through the alphabetic principle that students learn the interrelationships between letter-sound (grapheme-phoneme) correspondences, phonemic awareness, and early decoding skills (such as sounding out and blending letter sounds).

33. C: By definition, morphology is the identification and use of morphemes such as root words and affixes. Listening comprehension refers to the processes involved in understanding spoken language. Word consciousness refers to the knowledge required for students to learn and effectively utilize language. Textual analysis is an approach that researchers use to gain information and describe the characteristics of a recorded or visual message.

34. D: Print awareness includes all of the answer choices except the spelling of sight words. Print awareness includes Choice *A*, the differentiation of uppercase and lowercase letters, so that students can understand which words begin a sentence. Choice *B*, the identification of word boundaries, is also included in print awareness; that is, students should be made aware that words are made up of letters and that spaces appear between words, etc. Choice *C*, the proper tracking of words, is also included in print awareness, which is the realization that print is organized in a particular way, so books must be tracked and held accordingly.

35. D: Option I, word boundaries, is one of the factors modeled because as teachers point to individual words, they indicate separation between the words. Directionality is the ability to track words as they are being read, so this is also modeled. One-to-one correspondence, the last factor listed, is the ability to match written letters to words to spoken words when reading. It is another thing teachers model when they point to words while they read.

36. B: Structural analysis focuses on the meaning of morphemes. Morphemes include base words, prefixes, and word endings (inflections and suffixes) that are found within longer words. Students can use structural analysis skill to find familiar word parts within an unfamiliar word in order to decode the word and determine the definition of the new word. The prefix *im-* (meaning not) in the word *improbable* can help students derive the definition of an event that is not likely to occur.

37. B: The student is performing at the phonetic stage. Phonetic spellers will spell a word as it sounds. The speller perceives and represents all of the phonemes in a word. However, because phonetic spellers have limited sight word vocabulary, irregular words are often spelled incorrectly.

38. A: The teacher should have the student use a think-aloud to verbalize the directions of the shapes used when writing each letter. During think-alouds, teachers voice the metacognitive process that occurs when writing each part of a given letter. Students should be encouraged to do likewise when practicing writing the letters.

39. D: Teachers should capitalize on the transfer of relevant skills from the learner's original language(s). In this way, extra attention and instructional emphasis can be applied toward the teaching of sounds and meanings of words that are nontransferable between the two languages.

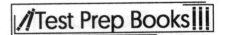

40. A: The identification of morphemes within words occurs during the instruction of structural analysis. Structural analysis is a word recognition skill that focuses on the meanings of word parts, or morphemes, during the introduction of a new word. Choice *B*, syllabic analysis, is a word analysis skill that helps students split words into syllables. Choice *C*, phonics, is the direct correspondence between and blending of letters and sounds. Choice *D*, the alphabetic principle, teaches that letters or other characters represent sounds.

41. B: Homophones are words that are pronounced the same way but differ in meaning and/or spelling. To and too are homophones because they are pronounced the same way but differ in both meaning and spelling. Choices *A*, *C*, and *D* are not homophones because they do not sound the same when spoken aloud.

42. B: The creation of word walls, Choice *I*, is advantageous during the phonetic stage of spelling development. On a word wall, words that share common consonant-vowel patterns or letter clusters are written in groups. Choices *II* and *III*, daily reading and writing opportunities, are also important in spelling instructions. Students need daily opportunities in order to review and practice spelling development. Daily journals or exit tickets are cognitive writing strategies effective in helping students reflect on what they have learned. Therefore, the correct answer, Choice *B*, includes all three answer options.

43. B: Nursery rhymes are used in kindergarten to develop phoneme recognition. Rhyming words are often almost identical except for their beginning letter(s), so rhyming is a great strategy to implement during the analytic phase of phoneme development.

44. B: Fluency is the ability to read automatically, recognizing words through subconscious phonetic processes. Automatic reading is how most adults read, decoding words without consciously sounding out every letter. Choice *A* is wrong because reading fluency has nothing to do with one's first language. Choice *C* is incorrect because even fluent readers make some mistakes. Choice *D* refers to self-correcting, not reading fluency.

45. B: DRTA, or directed reading thinking activity, incorporates both read-alouds and think-alouds. During a DRTA, students make predictions about the text at hand in order to set a purpose for reading, give cognitive focus, and activate prior knowledge. Students use reading comprehension in order to verify their predictions.

46. D: Boldfaced, highlighted, or italicized text notifies a student when a new vocabulary word or idea is present. Subtitles and headings can also alert a student to a change in topic or idea. These features are also important when answering questions, as a student may be able to easily find the answer with these typographic features present.

47. A: "Text evidence" refers to taking phrases and sentences directly from the text and writing them in the answer. Students are not asked to paraphrase, nor use any other resources to address the answer. Therefore, Choices *B*, *C*, and *D* are incorrect.

48. D: Group-based discussions, like think-pair-share, encourage all students to speak rather than having just one student share an answer. Each student is given time to collaborate with another student and share their thoughts. It is not intended for one student to give another student the answers, which is why Choice *C* is incorrect. Although Choices *A* and *B* might be correct, they are not the MOST important reason that group-based discussions are useful in the classroom.

142

49. C: A phoneme is the smallest individual unit of sound (for example, the phonogram "ph" represents the phoneme /f/). Choice *A*, a word, is typically composed of multiple phonemes. Choice *B* refers to phonics, and Choice *D* is a subtype of phoneme.

50. A: Scaffolding, as a strategy, provides a framework (as scaffolding would for a structure) to enable building around a foundation. In this way, providing cultural references enables students to make connections and build on existing knowledge. Choice *B* is incorrect; collaborative learning in this regard refers to students working together to learn language and new vocabulary. Discourse refers to conversation with another student as another example of collaborative learning, so Choice *C* is incorrect. Finally, Choice *D* is incorrect. Relevance has more to do with the importance of the student's new culture and the knowledge they gain around vocabulary and why it's important in the English language or American culture.

51. C: Morphemic analysis involves the breaking down of words into smaller parts that have meaning and using those meanings to put together enough information to understand the meaning of the larger word. Choice *A* is incorrect because contextual analysis requires that students look at the context of the word, how it's used, and sentence structures to learn the meaning through context. Etymological analysis, Choice *B*, refers to the history and origin of the full word or, sometimes, the root word itself, so it is incorrect. Choice *D* is incorrect because, like context, inferential analysis requires the student to infer what a word means based on the sentences around it and the overall meaning of the passage.

52. D: Students who struggle with comprehension may further be stymied by encountering words they are unfamiliar with in their readings. For those learners, providing a list of vocabulary words will improve their comprehension and help them build confidence in their reading abilities. Choice *A* is incorrect because vocabulary is focused on language knowledge rather than spelling. Choice *B* is incorrect. A vocabulary list will increase their familiarity with the meaning of the word and perhaps its recognition, but it will not speed up their reading if they are encountering it for the first time. Choice *C* is incorrect as well. Both groups of students will be required to use the dictionary for this assignment. Regardless of whether a student looks up the word before or after reading, the same dictionary skills will be required.

53. C: Asking oneself a comprehension question is a metacognition skill. Readers with metacognitive skills have learned to think about thinking. It gives students control over their learning while they read. KWL charts help students to identify what they already know about a given topic.

54. C: Choice *C* is correct. Discussing pre-reading techniques such as SQ3R would be the best reading strategy to focus on first. While Choice *A* and Choice *D* would prepare students for encountering unfamiliar words and understanding them better, it would not best prepare them for comprehending the entire text. Choice *B* is a good strategy for familiarizing students with the subject matter afterward, but Choice *C* best covers a comprehension strategy before reading a text.

55. A: Choice *A* is correct. Extensive reading is intended to improve fluency. Because the exercise asks students to read at or below grade level, comprehension, Choice *B*, and vocabulary, Choice *C*, should not be challenging. Automaticity, Choice *D*, is incorrect. A certain level of automaticity is expected at this point as the reading material is not challenging.

56. B: Choice *B* is correct. The ability to recount the content of a text and summarize it constitutes literal understanding. Inferential, Choice *A*, and evaluative, Choice *C*, levels of understanding require that students be able to read more deeply and infer implied information as well as compare and supplement

143

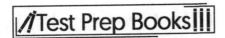

with their own existing knowledge. While analysis, Choice *D*, is introduced as a skill for literary readings, it's not a level of understanding.

57. A: Choice *A* is correct. Because an in-depth reading is required, one that requires students to comprehend at deeper levels, choosing subject matter that they are interested in is an important strategy. Ideally, there's an opportunity to challenge readers with new words and ideas for analysis, so Choice *B* is incorrect. While Choice *C* is an added benefit, it's not a reason to choose a specific story. Choice *D* is incorrect because, although literary texts may use academic language and structure, it's not a good reason to select a specific story.

58. A: Choice *A* is correct. A list of words pulled from a text are taken out of context, and so Choice *C* is incorrect. While intensive reading includes texts that have challenging words and ideas, reading them in context is one of the goals of that strategy, so Choice *B* is incorrect. While some of these words may be transferable, Choice *D* is not the best answer as demonstrating how and where they are transferable would be a better lesson. In other words, presenting students with a second, non–social studies text that used those words would be beneficial.

59. A: Choice *A* is correct. Section headings provide students with an outline of the content. Section headings also suggest which questions might be answered in the text. While images, Choice *B*, are helpful, they may not provide enough information. The end questions, Choice *C*, are a great tool, but they should be used as a supplement. The end questions may contain confusing details in the incorrect choices. Choice *D* is also incorrect. While the title is helpful, it's usually too broad to provide much information.

60. C: Choice *C* is correct. While Choice *A* would be a great activity after reading, it's not a good pre-reading choice. Choice *B* is too vague, and with no context it may prove to have minimal value. Choice *D* would be a good activity to include after reading to provide a different telling of the story. However, learning about the background of the diary is better preparation, Choice *C*.

61. D: Teachers use directed reading-thinking activities before and after reading to improve critical thinking and reading comprehension. Metacognitive skills are when learners think about their thinking. Self-monitoring is when children are asked to think as they read and ask themselves if what they have just read makes sense. KWL charts help guide students to identify what they already know about a given topic.

62. B: Choice *B* is correct. When a teacher is introducing new material that may include unfamiliar words or concepts, steering students toward important information is a useful strategy. It prepares them for the content as well as the language. While Choice *A* is a possibility, there's no indication that the questions will focus on vocabulary. Choice *C* is incorrect; reading academic language right before reading a historical event text will not help the students to answer the questions. Choice *D* is incorrect; usually questions are prepared by students after reading the text. Reading questions will not help them in creating their own questions in this scenario.

63. D: Choice *D* is correct. Early learners and readers are not yet at the inferential level of reading or the evaluative level, so the best strategy is to ask them how the story relates to them, which starts them thinking beyond the story itself. Choice *A* is a bit too complex for a first introduction. Choice *B* and Choice *C* both reflect literal understanding, but an analysis is trying to get the student to move beyond "just the facts."

64. B: Choice *B* is correct. Having students make up their own story about what the idiom means helps them to identify why the analogy works from idiomatic language to literal meaning. Looking up the literal definition does not help significantly with many idioms. Students may already know these words, so Choice *A* is incorrect. Sharing other idioms about food, Choice *C*, is a great activity, but only after students have discussed the meaning of "spill the beans." Choice *D* may provide some insight into the derivation of the saying, but it is a discussion for later.

65. A: Choice *A* is correct. Organizing foreign words by theme, Choice *A*, helps students think of words they already know. While co-teaching a lesson with a foreign language teacher, Choice *B*, would be great, it's more appropriate for an advanced lesson. Choice *C* is incorrect because, without a frame of reference, many students would not make the necessary connections or possibly even know what the words had in common. Many would likely understand or know some of the words, so this strategy would not be useful. Choice *D* is also incorrect because it would be more appropriate for an activity after students have been introduced to the concept and have learned to recognize foreign words in English.

66. D: Choice *D* is correct. Kinesthetic learners respond best to movement and tactile activities, so including movement in this exercise will engage them. In contrast, auditory learners, Choice *A*, and visual learners, Choice *C*, will respond better to aural and visual lessons, respectively. Choice *B* is incorrect as ELLs may have difficulty with word recognition nor is this activity specifically targeting their needs.

67. C: Choice *C* is correct. There are three primary goals for selecting vocabulary words: they should be important, transferable, and useful for continued study (of other words). Choice *A*, which includes known words, is unnecessary. Vocabulary lists should introduce new words or words to which students have had minimal exposure. Similarly, Choice *B* is incorrect as those words would not be transferable. Choice *D* is also incorrect as they are not, at that time, important.

68. C: Choice *C* is correct. Intensive reading is challenging reading that requires students to analyze vocabulary, syntax, and context clues to understand the text. While intensive reading necessarily involves interacting with the text, Choice *A*, it is not the primary goal. Teaching students how to use reference books, Choice *B*, may be useful, but that is not the primary goal of intensive reading. Preparing students for literary analysis, Choice *D*, is also incorrect, though it may be a secondary objective.

69. A: There is a positive correlation between a student's exposure to text and the academic achievement of that individual. Therefore, students should be given ample opportunities to read as much text as possible independently in order to gain vocabulary and background knowledge.

70. B: Inferential comprehension means the ability to understand the author's implied meaning (e.g., the fact that a character never has enough to eat suggests that he or she is struggling financially, even if the author never explicitly states this fact) and relate the reading to background knowledge. Choice *A*, literal comprehension, means understanding the plot of a literary text (e.g., what a character does) or the claims of an informational text (e.g., a fact about grasshoppers). Choice *C*, evaluative comprehension, is the ability to analyze a text and decide whether it is trustworthy. Evaluative comprehension involves critical-thinking skills, such as the ability to critique the author's argument and use of evidence or to recognize that the author may be biased. Choice *D* does not exist.

71. D: A guiding question is given before the reading or lesson to help students look for important information. Guiding questions keep students on track during readings because they know what to look

for. For example, a teacher might give students guiding questions such as "What three main points does the author make?" or "How would you critique the author's argument?" Choice *A*, a question and answer given together so students can check their work, is not necessarily given before the reading; additionally, teachers usually do not give answers for guiding questions. Choice *B* is incorrect because guiding questions are not necessarily rhetorical. Choice *C* refers to self-generated questions.

72. A: Evaluating the author's logic and evidence and distinguishing facts from beliefs are necessary for close reading of informational texts, which involves paying attention to every detail and analyzing its logic and claims. Choices *B*, *C*, and *D* all include close-reading techniques for literary texts; the question specifies informational texts. Literary devices, mapping the plot, and evaluating characterization and setting do not apply to expository texts, because informational texts do not typically have these features.

73. C: Students should be reading most assigned readings for total comprehension, so skimming is not adequate. Choice *A* is valid because skimming is useful for identifying keywords and determining whether a text is relevant. Choice *B* is valid because Grace is reading for pleasure and does not need to remember every detail. Choice *D* is a good strategy because cross-referencing texts is an ideal way to compare two related works.

74. B: Self-questioning refers to asking yourself questions and trying to answer them. Choice *A* is a kind of summarization, and Choice *C* is a level of comprehension. Choice *D* refers to questions the teacher gives out before a reading to help students notice important information so they can fully comprehend the material.

75. D: The student has broken the family Felidae into two subfamilies and noted species within the two. This kind of visual organization is called *semantic mapping,* and it provides a way for students to remember information by breaking it into groups and subgroups (e.g., in the question, the group Felidae is broken into the subgroups large and small cats, and these subgroups are further divided into smaller subgroups). Choice *A* is a misnomer for either semantic mapping or plot mapping. Choice *B* does not necessarily involve mapping the information, and Choice *C* involves mapping the timing of events rather than types and subtypes.

76. C: Text features are textual elements that supplement the main text by clarifying it, and indexes and glossaries are both text features. Graphic features are charts, graphs, etc., that visually represent the text. Choice *II* refers to formatting, and Choice *III* means literary devices, not text features.

77. C: Modeling involves the teacher walking students through their own thought process so they learn how and when to use comprehension strategies. Choices *A* and *D* refer to discussion, and Choice *B* is about mapping and visualization rather than modeling.

78. A: Because Andrea is teaching her students to track their own thought processes, she is teaching metacognition. Choice *B* means asking yourself questions about the text, and Choice *C* is a way of charting information into a diagram. Choice *D* means being able to calm and control your own emotions.

79. D: A schema is a framework or structure that stores and retrieves multiple, interrelated learning elements as a single packet of knowledge. Children who have greater exposure to life events have greater schemas. Thus, students who bring extensive background knowledge to the classroom are likely to experience easier automation when reading. In this way, background knowledge and reading

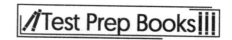

comprehension are directly related. Likewise, students who have greater background knowledge are able to learn a greater number of new concepts at a faster rate.

80. C: A student's reading ability will most likely differ when assessed via a reading assessment versus a writing sample. There are five types of vocabulary: listening, speaking, written, sight, and meaning. Most often, listening vocabulary contains the greatest number of words. This is usually followed by speaking vocabulary, sight reading vocabulary, meaning vocabulary, and written vocabulary. Formal written language usually utilizes a richer vocabulary than everyday oral language. Thus, students show differing strengths in reading vocabulary and writing vocabulary.

81. B: Informal reading assessments allow teachers to create differentiated assessments that target reading skills of individual students. In this way, teachers can gain insight into a student's reading strengths and weaknesses. Informal assessments can help teachers decide what content and strategies need to be targeted. However, standardized reading assessments provide all students with the same structure to assess multiple skills at one time. Standardized reading assessments cannot be individualized. Such assessments are best used for gaining an overview of student reading abilities.

82. D: Word-reading accuracy is often measured by counting the number of errors that occur per 100 words of oral reading. This information is used to select the appropriate level of text for an individual.

83. B: Differentiated instruction acknowledges that, while a group of students may be learning the same subject, the way each student learns and processes the subject is different. **It** involves looking at the different learning methods and reading areas and identifying which ones students respond to. Educators can then tailor, or differentiate, lessons to build on these skills and expedite the learning process. Choice *A* is incorrect for two reasons. One, it is impossible to teach different subjects to each student in a classroom simultaneously. Two, there are some subjects, such as reading, that students must learn even if they have no interest initially. It is the teacher's job to find ways to interest students in the subject matter. Choice *C* is incorrect because, while intervention groups may be a useful method of differentiated instruction, it is not the best description. Choice *D* is incorrect for the same reason – using a wide variety of learning resources is very helpful for differentiated instruction, but it is not the best description of differentiated instruction.

84. A: Summative assessments are formal assessments that are given at the end of a unit of study. These assessments are usually longer in length. They are not completed daily. These summative assessments shouldn't be confused with informal assessments, which are used more frequently to determine mastery of the day's objective. However, summative assessments may be used to determine students' mastery in order to form intervention groups thereafter.

85. A: Assessments should always be frequent and ongoing for all students, but especially for those with special needs. These assessments may be informal but should be given daily after direct instruction and modeling. While summative assessments are important, they should not be the first and only assessment during a unit of study; usually summative assessments come at the end of a unit. Weekly and monthly assessments are too infrequent for remediation, intervention, or identification of struggling areas.

86. C: Writing samples are the most appropriate assessment of spelling for students who are performing at the pre-phonetic stages. During this stage, students participate in pre-communicative writing, which appears to be a jumble of letter-like forms rather than a series of discrete letters. Samples

of students' pre-communicative writing can be used to assess their understanding of the alphabetic principle and their knowledge of letter-sound correspondences.

87. A: Phonological awareness is best assessed through identification of rimes or onsets within words. Instruction of **phonological awareness** includes detecting and identifying word boundaries, onsets/rimes, syllables, and rhyming words.

88. B: High-frequency words are taught during the instruction of sight word recognition. Sight words, sometimes referred to as high-frequency words, are words that are used often but may not follow the regular principles of phonics. Sight words may also be defined as words that students are able to recognize and read without having to sound out.

89. C: Decoding should be assessed in context in addition to isolation. To assess in context, students read passages from appropriate texts aloud to the teacher so that the teacher can analyze their approach to figuring out unknown words. Decoding should also be assessed in isolation. In these types of assessments, students are given a list of words and/or phonics patterns. Initially, high-frequency words that follow predictable phonics patterns are presented. The words that are presented become more challenging as a student masters less difficult words.

90. D: Sight vocabulary refers to the words a person can correctly recognize and pronounce when reading. Poor word recognition, insufficient background knowledge, or an insufficient amount of content vocabulary can all affect someone's sight vocabulary. Correct pronunciation can influence a person's skill in spelling a specific word, but the opposite is less likely, as most people can still pronounce words well even if they don't spell it correctly.

91. B: Because digital texts often offer vocabulary supports such as pop-up dictionaries, they are ideal for vocabulary-heavy readings. Choices *A* and *C* are incorrect because digital texts can actually create tracking problems, especially when there are few paragraph breaks. Choice *D* is incorrect because digital texts are a good way to make it easy for students to use online reference materials (charts, summaries, etc.) while reading.

92. B: The instructional level is the level of text students can generally read and understand but need some help to fully comprehend. It is called the *instructional level* because it is best used in class when teachers are available to help, not in independent readings when students will be by themselves and struggle. Because the instructional level runs from 70% to 85% comprehension accuracy, Krista falls within it. Choice *A*, the independent level at which students can read the text entirely by themselves, demands more than 90% comprehension accuracy. Choice *C*, the frustration level, is composed of texts the student comprehends with less than 70% accuracy and should not read at all. Finally, Choice *D* represents texts the student can comprehend with more than 70% accuracy when he or she hears them read aloud. These texts are great when teachers or parents read them to students, but students should not read them themselves because they are too difficult.

93. C: If a test is valid, it can accurately measure students' skills and weaknesses. If a test is reliable, a student who is staying at the same reading level could take the test multiple times and receive the same or very similar scores. Choice *A* gives the wrong definition of *accuracy,* Choice *B* reverses the factors, and Choice *D* gives the definition of *reliability* for *validity* and has a completely wrong answer for *reliability.*

148

94. A: Individual testing is best for flexible testing that determines the details of students' skills and supports students. Because Choice *B* describes a scenario in which the teacher wants to give the same test to all the students, individual testing is not necessary. Choices *C* and *D* both describe students who are old enough to read for themselves and are being tested on non-oral skills, and therefore, individual testing is not necessary.

95. C: The Lexile Text Measure is a leveling system that provides a database of texts ranked by difficulty. Although Choice *A* determines complexity, it does not level text. Choices *B* and *D* are unrelated.

96. B: Decodable text is text that is 100% composed of letters or words the students have studied; theoretically, the students should be able to read it without running into anything they do not understand. Choice *A* refers to text separated into syllables, which may still contain unfamiliar sounds. Choice *C* describes child-friendly formatting, and Choice *D* refers to built-in glossaries/dictionaries in digital texts.

97. C: The frustration level is composed of text that is far too difficult for the student. Teachers should avoid this type of text. The frustration level is defined by comprehension scores lower than 70% and reading accuracy scores below 90%: because Carson's scores are well below these benchmarks, he is definitely in the frustration level. Choices *A*, *B*, and *D* all require comprehension above 70%, and Choice *D* is an auditory test and therefore does not involve any reading score.

98. C: The concrete operational stage is the third of Jean Piaget's developmental stages. These stages are a way of understanding children's cognitive development. As children age, they begin to think more symbolically (i.e., understanding that one thing can stand for another) and learn to use logic more adeptly. Concrete operational children are between the ages of 7 and 11 and understand conservation, which is the understanding that the same amount of a substance can look different when it is in different forms (for instance, a piece of play dough will look different when it is in a ball than when it is flattened). Choice *A* refers to babies younger than 2 years old. Choice *B* means children between the ages of 2 and 7; a child in this stage would not yet understand conservation. Choice *D* means children who are older than 11 and can use logic proficiently.

99. D: The integrated approach is an approach to reading that mixes phonics with some sight words. Choice *A* refers to sight words alone, and Choice *B* refers to phonics alone. Choice *C* is a misnomer for the integrated approach.

100. B: Multisensory educations helps children learn by maximizing the pathways to learning. For example, instead of just seeing letters, children could feel letter cutouts to learn their shapes. Choices *A* and *C* might be true in some situations, but these answers are not the reason teachers use multisensory education. Choice *D* does not make sense because sensorimotor children are younger than 2 years old, and multisensory education is useful for children at any age.

Dear OAE Test Taker,

Thank you for purchasing this study guide for your OAE Foundations of Reading exam. We hope that we exceeded your expectations.

Our goal in creating this study guide was to cover all of the topics that you will see on the test. We also strove to make our practice questions as similar as possible to what you will encounter on test day. With that being said, if you found something that you feel was not up to your standards, please send us an email and let us know.

We have study guides in a wide variety of fields. If you're interested in one, try searching for it on Amazon or send us an email.

Thanks Again and Happy Testing!
Product Development Team
info@studyguideteam.com

FREE Test Taking Tips Video/DVD Offer

To better serve you, we created videos covering test taking tips that we want to give you for FREE. **These videos cover world-class tips that will help you succeed on your test.**

We just ask that you send us feedback about this product. Please let us know what you thought about it—whether good, bad, or indifferent.

To get your **FREE videos**, you can use the QR code below or email freevideos@studyguideteam.com with "Free Videos" in the subject line and the following information in the body of the email:

    a. The title of your product

    b. Your product rating on a scale of 1-5, with 5 being the highest

    c. Your feedback about the product

If you have any questions or concerns, please don't hesitate to contact us at info@studyguideteam.com.

Thank you!

Made in the USA
Monee, IL
09 July 2024

61523256R00090